*How Guys Really Think and How to Get
the Right One Interested in You*

*Why
Hasn't
He
Called?*

Matt Titus and Tamsen Fadal

McGraw Hill

D0377615

New York   Chicago   San Francisco   Lisbon   London   Madrid   Mexico City
Milan   New Delhi   San Juan   Seoul   Singapore   Sydney   Toronto

The *McGraw·Hill* Companies

Library of Congress Cataloging-in-Publication Data

Titus, Matt.
  Why hasn't he called? : how guys really think and how to get the right one interested in you / Matt Titus and Tamsen Fadal.
       p.   cm.
  Includes index.
  ISBN-13: 978-0-07-154609-6 (alk. paper)
  ISBN-10:   0-07-154609-X
  1. Man-woman relationships.   2. Men—Psychology.   3. Women—Psychology.
4. Dating (Social customs)   I. Fadal, Tamsen.   II. Title.

  HQ801.T499   2008
  646.7'7082—dc22   2007049514

    2 3 4 5 6 7 8 9 10 11 12 13 14 15 16 17 18 19 20 21   FGR/FGR   0 9 8

ISBN 978-0-07-154609-6
MHID   0-07-154609-X

Interior design by Monica Baziuk
Illustrations by Eddie Varley

McGraw-Hill books are available at special quantity discounts to use as premiums and sales promotions or for use in corporate training programs. To contact a representative, please visit the Contact Us pages at www.mhprofessional.com.

This book is printed on acid-free paper.

To my late mother, Libby, who taught me
how to love and how to be loved.

And, to my father, Jim, and my brother Cristan, who
are my rocks in life and made me who I am today.

And to my loving husband, Matt, who gives
me love, support, and inspiration every day as
my partner and my best friend in life.

—TAMSEN

To my late mother, Faith, whom I wish
could have seen me become a man.

And to my father, Paul, who is not only a sup-
portive dad but also a friend.

Last but not least, to my loving wife, Tamsen, whose energy
and love are never ending. You have changed my life forever.

—MATT

CONTENTS

ACKNOWLEDGMENTS

THE WORLD of dating may be crazy, but we would like to thank the people who kept us sane for the love of this book. We could not have done it without the dedication and generosity of your time and effort, and we thank you from the bottom of our hearts.

None of this would have been possible without the creative inspiration of our illustrator and best friend, Eddie Varley, who not only gets our voice but also helps us bring it to life.

Thank you to Bonnie Bauman, our editor, who shaped and focused our ideas and words. And a special thank-you to our literary agent, Carol Mann, who believed in us and our vision and found us a perfect home at McGraw-Hill.

To Johanna Bowman and Deborah Brody and all the folks at McGraw-Hill—thank you for having the faith in us to do this book.

To Karen Kelly, David Kelly, Marta Tracy, Rob Pearson, and Dianna and Mike Feldman, you stood by us every step of the way as this book was being written, and we are forever grateful.

To our loving families and friends, especially Carol and Jennifer Fadal, who patiently read one rough draft after another of *Why Hasn't He Called?*—thank you for your love, patience, and support.

We must add, we couldn't have done it without all those countless cans of Rockstar Energy Drink that got us through the late hours!

And a huge kiss to Matsen and Parker, our Chihuahuas, who sat patiently on our laps while we spent weeks writing this book instead of walking them in Central Park! We promise we'll make it up to you.

Finally, to all the people who have worked with us and who have shared their dating breakups and makeups, our one true hope is that you find the love and happiness you deserve.

INTRODUCTION

WHO WE ARE: MATT TITUS

AND TAMSEN FADAL

• • • • • • • • • • • • MEET MATT • • • • • • • • • • • • •

I was the ultimate player. Case in point: as I was being lifted onto a CT scan machine in the emergency room, I still had enough "player" running through my veins to pull a trauma technician down to my lips and whisper into his ear, "Buddy, you've got to help me out. My wife is in the waiting room, and my girlfriend is on her way. Please get ahold of my girlfriend and tell her I'm OK and not to come to the hospital and I will call her soon." This was coming from a guy who had, twenty minutes earlier, been in a near-fatal motorcycle accident. I had hit rock bottom.

Here's my story.

I owned a medical spa and a chain of personal training gyms. I had been having an affair with my nutritionist for the past six months and had what we called "client evaluations" planned that night at her place. I had told my lovely, devoted wife that I had an investor meeting and would be home by 10:00 P.M. This didn't give me a lot of time. This wasn't the first time I had been unfaithful to my wife, but it certainly was the most challenging. Play had become work. As any serial adulterer well knows, you can't "have sex and run," even if it's with your girlfriend on the side. My girlfriend didn't seem to mind playing the role of the other woman, but when she was treated disrespectfully, the situation became completely unacceptable to her. So, in order to get what I wanted, I had to treat her like a lady, even though she was sleeping with a married man. What planet was I living on? There I was, having to get over to her apartment, take her out to dinner (at some secluded place), and then finally get back to her apartment for what brought me there in the first place: sex. Now remember, I had to accomplish all of this within a span of three hours. I, of course, made my necessary diversion call to my innocent wife to tell her I was on my way to the investor meeting and would be home later. Every time I did this, my self-loathing would start to creep up to the surface, but I would immediately push it back down by saying to myself: "This will be the last time." Aren't men pathetic?

I certainly was.

The traffic light was more yellow than red, so I accelerated straight through the intersection. Unfortunately, the car waiting at the light saw green and turned in front of me. I immediately locked up my back wheel, which only seemed to increase my acceleration toward the car. Being an inexperienced rider, I panicked and locked up the front brake. I was thrown over the handlebars thirty feet through the air. My helmet flew off, and my body smashed into the front of the oncoming car. After I bounced off the front of the car, my bike, having dutifully followed me through the intersection, provided me the comfortable landing cushion of a burning exhaust pipe. The injuries I received on the road that day, both physically and emotionally, left me scarred forever.

So there I was, dazed, lying on a burning exhaust pipe with a punctured lung and five broken ribs, all for a little "tail" on the side! What an idiot!

You would think this accident would have been one of those "life-altering moments" you hear about on TV. Not for my poor lost soul. Instead, the following week I devoted my energy to coordinating hospital visits between my wife and my girlfriend.

Broken ribs, a nasty third-degree burn, and a punctured lung didn't stop me from lying to my wife about the actual time of my hospital discharge a week later. I told her I would be discharged at the end of the day when in fact I was getting sprung at 1:00 P.M. Thanks to this little lie, I would have just enough time to have my girlfriend pick me up and take me to her apartment before I went home to my wife. I can still recall the excruciating pain of freshly broken ribs coupled with the burning sensation of a recent skin graft being stretched as I desperately tried to make out with her. But my physical injuries were minor compared to the condition of my mind. Despite the fact that I knew I was putting everything at risk with my behavior, I couldn't stop my deceitful ways.

Just as I predicted, I lost it all. Three months later, I woke up and simply had had enough. It was a weekend I'll never forget. My wife was in the kitchen making me breakfast. She looked so content just being my wife. She had no idea what was really going on. The concept of lying and cheating was so foreign to her that it was never even a passing thought in her mind. The longer I watched her, the more I loathed myself. Why was I doing this to such a beautiful person who deserved so much more? She deserved what I wasn't: a man who cherished everything about her and was truly committed to her in every imaginable way. I had to stop being so selfish and let her go. If I was going to live my life as a loser, it should affect only me. In one moment, the sheer weight of my constant lies and infidelities became too much for me to bear. I confessed everything. When I saw the pain and anguish reflected in her eyes, I vowed never to cause anyone that kind of heartache again.

My marriage ended in that moment. I left my wife for my girlfriend. Not surprisingly, that also had a hideous ending. Because I felt responsible for my failed marriage, I left my wife with everything we had. I was going to start over with the person I thought was the "true love of my life." Unfortunately, I had made a critical error in my soul-mate selection process.

The truth was my relationship with my girlfriend had no real substance. It was based purely on endorphins and adrenaline from sneaking around. In only three months, I realized that my "soul mate" was totally wrong for me. The relationship ended. Badly. I had no wife. I had no girlfriend. I had no money. My "wheels" were a bicycle.

In the days and weeks that followed, I lived on my friend's couch haunted nightly by my past lies, cheating, and indiscretions. At night I would look out into the darkness of the city and feel an icy cold loneliness that I'd never experienced in my life.

One night, I was riding home from work in the pouring rain. I was in the middle of the road, on my bicycle, competing with trucks and buses for road space, while sort of hoping one of them would slide into me and end my misery. I was in what seemed like unbearable emotional pain. I missed my best friend (my ex-wife), and I was riddled with guilt. There are certain moments in a person's life that are monumental in creating new frontiers and promises of change, and this was one of mine. As the rain pelted my face and cars sped past me at precariously close distances, I vowed to never be disrespectful, deceitful, or unfaithful to another woman.

Much time has passed since that rainy night years ago. Not only have I kept my promise to never disrespect, deceive, or cheat on a woman, but I also have made it my life's mission to help women understand men. I've done this by integrating a matchmaking service into my already established personal fitness business. The marriage of the two (pardon the pun) came about when I realized while helping my clients look their best that many of them had extremely unfulfilling love lives. I noticed that a lot of them were either clueless when it came to understanding the opposite sex or simply made bad choices when selecting a significant other. I knew that with my first-hand, real-life experiences I could be of help.

Over time more people learned about my service as a dating coach. My only credentials were my real-life relationship experiences. My coaching strategy simply involved telling clients what I had done right, what I had done wrong, and what I had learned along the way. Nonetheless, people took my advice with positive results. It wasn't long before I started introducing my clients to each other, people they otherwise would not have met. Many of the matches were a success. My clients told their friends about the service, and soon people were lining up outside my door to receive solid relationship coaching and be set up with a potential partner. Matt's Little Black Book (MLBB), a boutique matchmaking service, was born.

Then I met Tamsen. (I'll let her give you the details.) We are truly partners in every way. Tamsen and I have what I consider to be all of the ingredients of a successful relationship. We are both willing to make compromises, and I truly respect her for her intelligence and constant drive to better herself. It's that drive and intelligence that keeps me on my toes and ensures I'll never get bored with her. Not to mention the fact that I'm incredibly attracted to her. I will happily chase her for the rest of my life. It's all there, and this time it feels so right. As for my ex-wife, she is happily remarried to a wonderful guy, and they have two beautiful children.

It has now been four years since I founded MLBB. In that time I have introduced nearly two thousand men and women, and I am proud to say that my service has been responsible for many lasting relationships and numerous happy marriages.

Luckily for me, Tamsen decided to hop on board and help me steer my clients in the right direction. Together, Tamsen and I will go to any lengths to help women understand the male mind. We have even made ourselves available to our clients twenty-four hours a day (via text messaging) to make sure they don't take a romantic misstep during the dating process. This service was introduced when one of our clients was out with a guy we matched her up with and started frantically texting us to ask if she should go back to his house for a "nightcap." The incident also planted the seed for another of our ventures: Sassybean.com.

Sassybean.com is a website that allows us to reach out to tens of thousands of women with a free weekly online magazine that addresses the most frequently asked questions women have regarding dating, relationships, and the craziness of the male mind. This weekly dose of dating, relationship, and lifestyle advice is accompanied by a whimsical illustration depicting the topic of the week. On the site, Tamsen and I deliver advice in a lighthearted, fun way that empowers women and makes them feel great about themselves.

Together, Tamsen and I face the same everyday challenges that all couples face. We fight, bicker, and make up just like everybody else. That's why we consider our advice to be better than "expert advice"—because it comes from a real couple. We truly love each other, and it is our hope that we can help others find the same love that we have found.

MEET TAMSEN

I was a successful reporter with an Emmy under my belt, and yet my dating life was a complete disaster. My lackluster dating luck followed me when I moved to Philadelphia for a top reporting job in television. Because I spent twenty-four hours a day at the office, I started to date guys who worked with me in one capacity or another—three at once. One of them I became involved with because I enjoyed having control over a very powerful man. The other two I dated for attention and out of convenience. I knew that each one of these guys was totally wrong for me, so there wasn't a chance for any emotional attachment. I basically dated guys I had no chance of a future with, but with whom I could pass the time and entertain myself. As I soon found out, this can turn into a dangerous game.

It all came to a head one night when I was sitting at my desk desperate to be by myself. Ironically, I craved solitude despite the fact that I was dating three men I really had no interest in to avoid being alone. As I sat at my desk, trying to prepare for my 11:00 P.M. broadcast, I heard Guy #1's voice and knew that I was going to have to think of a good excuse to avoid him. As I felt the hairs on the back of my neck stand up (what happens to us girls when we really don't want to be around a guy we are seeing), he whispered into my ear asking me to grab a late-night drink at his apartment. I somehow managed to smile and told him I would be there in an hour. Ugh. As I began to internally melt down, I was interrupted by the phone. I answered it without thinking, only to hear a very familiar voice on the other end of the line, Guy #2: "Hey, babe, isn't it cool to be able to see me when I talk to you? It's like our very own teleconference!" Our desks were within viewing distance of each other. Guy #2 was not quite as powerful as Guy #1, and not quite as smart, but he sure was cute. I managed to mutter that I was behind and needed to talk to him after the show. He said, "No problem, babe, we can talk over drinks tonight. Remember, it's Wednesday night, our date night. See you at 11:30." As I hung up the phone, I calculated the distance from my desk to the window and actually considering jumping. But I didn't have enough personal days for a full recovery. I was just about to look back down at my script when I was spun around in my chair and found myself face-to-face with Guy #3, who worked in yet another part of the building. He wanted to "talk," since I had not been answering his calls all week. He looked so desperate and upset there was no way that I could possibly get out of the coffee date that I agreed to for later that night. I thought to myself: "How did I get here?" I had no idea what I was doing, I was dating with the skill of a high school girl, and I was choosing men who were completely wrong for me.

By the time I reached my early thirties, I had an extremely successful career in television, wonderful girlfriends, and a jam-packed social calendar. But I had been so busy working and dating the wrong men that I had no true prospects in terms of a lifelong partner. Now don't get me wrong, I don't believe you have to have a man in your life to be happy. I spent years being very happy as a single, but suddenly I wanted something more. . . . Enter Matt.

I first met Matt while I was working in Philadelphia. There he was, great looking, successful, with a personality that could charm anyone. He and I had crossed paths several times at the openings of his medical spas, health clubs, and various businesses. He was a real man-about-town with a reputation for loving the ladies. However, recently through a pretty credible "source," I had heard he had taken some hard knocks. So, when he approached me in the gym and asked me out for coffee, what I saw in his piercing blue eyes was not the fast-talking womanizer that he was known as, but rather a true and sincere guy who had recently learned many tough life lessons.

Nevertheless, I put my guard up. I took his number and gave him mine without any promise of a future plan of getting together. I was still not sure if I was ready for a relationship. I thought if I was going to date him, I would proceed with caution. So I told him that I was still dating other guys and that he would have to know from the outset I would not be available unless he asked me out ahead of time.

Matt went after me with a vengeance. He would sit with me through dinners where I had to excuse myself three and four times to continue the juggling of my demanding suitors. He was so committed to proving himself that he walked me to a date I had with another guy! It was 11:30 P.M., I had just gotten off work, it was raining, and my date was just a few blocks away. Matt showed up with an umbrella and walked me there anyway. Talk about a man on a mission!

I never called Matt first. I saw him only once a week for the first month, and I never once asked myself, "Why hasn't he called?" That's because he was calling. And I wanted him to.

Before long, the other men I was dating fell by the wayside. I connected with Matt in a way that I never thought possible. All the while I continued to watch my coworkers and girlfriends make the same mistakes I had made pre-Matt. That's why I decided to jump into the fray with Matt so that together we could bring our lessons as a real couple to the masses. My role with MLBB is to provide male clients a look inside the ever-elusive female mind. On top of that, I give our female clients pointers on their appearance, demeanor, and behavior. In addition, I bring all my journalism and investigative skills to bear when evaluating clients. I am expert at discerning which men and women are really serious about finding a soul mate. If someone isn't ready for a relationship, we don't take that person on. I pitch in on Sassybean.com as well. Each day Matt and I sit together and answer dozens of e-mails from women (and some men) about how to date, love, or find happiness as a single. We try to make our advice empowering but firm when it comes to the dos and don'ts of dating, Matt's Secrets of the Boys Club, and tips on beauty and style.

• • • • • • • WHY HASN'T HE CALLED? • • • • • • •

My intention in this book is *not* to pontificate in a holier-than-thou way about what to do or not do while you work to be a sexy, savvy single, but rather to provide never-before-heard insight into the way men truly think and behave. I have worked with thousands of women who just want to be involved in a satisfying relationship. In this book, I plan to show you how to spot "players," how to determine the men who are serious about a relationship, and how to avoid the ones that should be written off as confirmed bachelors. It is my personal passion to work with Tamsen to guide you through the completely unpredictable and sometimes crazy world of dating. In doing so, I have become a "traitor" to my gender as I happily reveal all of the infamous Secrets of the Boys Club.

By the time you are finished reading *Why Hasn't He Called?* you will have learned the most important things all women need to know to become what I call a "power dater." This book will teach you where to go to meet the right kind of guys and how to successfully flirt to attract them. You will also gain a complete understanding of what men love to see on a first date as well as the missteps that will guarantee there won't be a second date. Among other topics, we will talk about how long you should wait to sleep with him. This book will put you one step ahead of men because it will teach you how they think and how to predict their actions.

 As a woman, I know that long after a date has ended us girls spend time trying to interpret his every move and ponder over every word he said. My aim in this book is to help women stop wasting time on the wrong guys and find the right ones. *Why Hasn't He Called?* will not only empower you when and if the phone doesn't ring, but will also ensure that you are never again looking for that blinking light on the answering machine or continuously checking your caller ID just to make sure you didn't miss the call.

After reading this book, you will have learned how to pick the men who do call and instantly forget about those who never had any intention of picking up the phone.

SECRETS OF THE BOYS CLUB

Somewhere in Manhattan a first date is taking place at a trendy lounge over drinks.

Here are the undisputed facts:

✦ Both parties are interested in each other on some level.
✦ They agreed on a time and location.

In the world of dating and relationships, this is about as far as undisputed facts go when it comes to a man and woman meeting for the first time.

We have her version and we have his version of the first date. Let's compare the two.

HER VERSION

He was right on time and already had a table. He must have called ahead because it was the best table in the place. That's thoughtful; he must think I'm special.

He looked really good. I wonder how he had time to go home, shower, shave, change clothes, and still get here on time. He did that all for me. Wow.

The conversation was effortless; he seemed to be interested in every word I had to say. He kept asking me if I needed anything more to drink—what a gentleman! He is so responsible; he told me that he only had until 10:00 P.M. because he had an early morning presentation. I love a guy with a career focus.

He mentioned his parents' upcoming twenty-five-year wedding anniversary, so he is definitely not opposed to marriage. When the date ended we even walked for a while, talking about anything that popped into our heads; it was so romantic. When it was time for him to go in the other direction, he looked me right in the eyes and told me he had had a great time and would call me soon. He leaned over to kiss me, and I turned my cheek. I never kiss on a first date, so he just smiled and said good night. What a wonderful end to a perfect date! I can't wait for him to call.

• • • • • • • • • • • • • HIS VERSION • • • • • • • • • • • • •

I was on my way home last night when I remembered that I had promised to meet this girl after work. I was going to cancel, but what the hell; you never know what could happen. Luckily, I had my overnight stuff in the trunk from the past weekend, which I spent romping with some chick I sleep with upstate. So, I grabbed my electric razor and ran it over my face and then put on a semiclean Polo shirt and my two-day-old jeans—not bad for changing in the backseat!

I actually got there ten minutes early. The place was packed, so I thought me and whatever-her-name-was would have to stand. Then I remembered: "Oh yeah, her name is Sheila, can't forget that. Damn!" I was about to walk up to the bar when I noticed how hot the hostess was, so I thought I would strike up a conversation. This girl was so awesome: in addition to giving me her number, she gave me the best table in the place.

Sheila showed up and yeah, she was attractive, but not as hot as I had remembered. God, what was I thinking when I agreed to this date? I must have been hammered. She talked so much I think that I went into a hyp-notic trance while I was staring her dead in the face. I tried to get her drunk, but she wasn't a drinker. I was in the flames of hell with a medi-ocre yapper.

I had no choice but to play the "big pre-sentation at work" card. It worked like a charm. I thought I would make a clean break until she kept following me almost back to my place. I couldn't lose her! Finally, I picked a random street that was close to my apartment, just to get away from her. When I stopped to say goodbye, she actually didn't look half bad. It must have been the streetlight hitting her face at just the right angle. So I thought, "What the hell, she probably doesn't look that bad from behind either." Maybe if I kissed her passionately, she might get turned on enough for me to take her back to my place. As I went to kiss her, she "cheeked" me. I couldn't believe it. Well, that was the last straw. I told her I'd give her a call . . . yeah right.

 Does this scenario sound familiar? It should, because it happens more times in the land of Singlesville than we care to admit. Every week, Tamsen and I talk to dozens of women who ask us the same questions over and over again: What is he thinking? Does he like me? WHY HASN'T HE CALLED?!

In this chapter you will become privy to some of the best-kept Secrets of the Boys Club, such as the two categories men use to define every woman they meet. (That's right, there are only two. We're not all that complicated.) In addition, we'll spend some time dissecting the first date described here to point out all of the red flags that were waving in that poor gal's face. Finally, we'll give you a cheat sheet that describes each of the different kinds of players you'll be up against as you take to the field. And throughout this chapter and the chapters that follow, whenever a potential pitfall crops up, we'll provide you with a tried-and-true *solution* to the dilemma.

· · · · · · WELCOME TO THE BOYS CLUB · · · · · ·

The first thing you should know about the Boys Club is that its members have a bond that is virtually unbreakable. Their loyalty to each other runs deeper than the deepest trenches of the ocean. Their code of silence rivals the famous cosa nostra mentality of the mob. They will lie, cheat, and steal on behalf of one another with the ease of an Enron exec. You'd think with all of the sacrifice, risk, and complete loyalty required of its members, the standards of admission would be higher than those of the Oval Office itself. Not so. The fact is the only membership requirement is having a "little member" of your own. That "little member" tends to control the men they are attached to and has the ability to take over all the thought processes of their hosts, especially when in close proximity to attractive females.

In all seriousness, men cover up for each other because it's in their genetic makeup to do so. Monogamy is a socially learned behavior that the male species does not readily embrace. Think about it. Historically, man's role has been to run around the forest and propagate the species by impregnating as many women as possible. With the introduction of "morality cages," such as monogamy, marriage, and commitment, men's instinctive sexual impulses are stopped dead in their tracks. For example, when a guy who is in a relationship sees another woman he would like to sleep with, his instinct to go after her is so strong it temporarily blocks out his morality. The good news is more mature guys are able to keep these thoughts tightly locked away in their "morality cages." Their thoughts never become actions. Now the bad news: this lockdown brings about a feeling of complete frustration. All guys experience this frustration. A common way to ease this feeling and rebel, while still keeping their own cages tightly locked up, is to help let a friend out of his "morality cage" for an affair or a one-night stand.

To sum it all up, the Boys Club is the product of male rebellious behavior that's a result of society trying to civilize and control the sexual instincts of a man. It's their common feelings of frustration that cause men to band together and assist each other by lying, cheating, or keeping silent in order to obtain the ultimate goal: sex with a girl who is neither wife nor girlfriend.

"WOULD SLEEP WITH" GIRLS VS. "WOULD NOT SLEEP WITH" GIRLS

Before we dissect "The First Date," let's take a quick step back in time to see where it all began. The caveman dwells in all modern men, and not so silently either. All the quick-witted humor, focused intellectual conversation, and sweeping romantic gestures are premeditated, strategic maneuvers used to attain one goal and one goal only: getting her into the cave. If men had it their way, there would be no dialogue, just a quick dragging into the cave followed by instant gratification. There would be no conversation, no sharing of emotions, just pure physical release. Yes, men have evolved; they walk upright and put on suits, but in most cases, that may be the extent of their evolution.

Now, I realize modern man is not running around with a *club* in his hand, but he is hanging out in *clubs* searching for the perfect cavewoman, which is often just as uncivilized. And here is what goes through a man's mind the first time he notices you. First, he immediately places you into one of two categories: "Would Sleep With" or "Would Not Sleep With." Once he decides you are in the "Would Sleep With" category, three more thoughts cross his mind:

1. What would she look like in my bed with her clothes on the floor?
2. What will her face look like when I kiss her?
3. How high maintenance will she be in a relationship, and can I deal with it?

The more attracted a guy is to a woman, the more effort he will put into making her happy. Men are blinded by their visual pleasures and will basically do anything to sleep with a beautiful woman. When a man is extremely sexually attracted to a woman, a testosterone response that supersedes all rational thought is immediately elicited. The resulting behavior has started wars (Helen of Troy), kicked off presidential impeachment hearings (Bill and Monica), and completely ruined many personal and professional lives ending in nasty divorces splashed across the front pages of newspapers.

Men deal with the women in the "Would Not Sleep With" category like families treat ugly stepchildren: as inconsequential burdens. In addition, men recover all sensibility and reason when dealing with women they are not sexually attracted to. Finally, these are the only women that men can successfully have as friends.

Here is another prehistoric secret of the Boys Club: men's actions can be totally controlled by the objects of their affection. The minute that a man sexually desires a woman, he is completely under her control. If she can seize this moment, she will always be in control of the relationship, as well as the man. A woman's sexuality is the single most powerful thing on earth; it can be a man's Kryptonite. In later chapters, Tamsen and I will explain how, once he does call, you can leverage your sexuality to have the most satisfying relationship possible.

••••• DISSECTING "THE FIRST DATE" •••••

Now it's time to dissect "The First Date" so that the next time you are on it, you will take strategic action instead of acting out of emotion. The woman we described earlier is still probably waiting at home for that loser to call. If she understood guys, she would have known that there was no chance he was ever going to call, or better yet, she wouldn't have even wanted him to call. Let's review. To her, the guy seemed to do all the right things. He was on time. He got a good table. He listened to her talk. But here are a few red flags he threw up that would have been obvious if she had only been looking out for them.

Red flag: He didn't say much.

Interpretation: She did the talking, most likely to keep the conversation going. But, the fact that he sat there and listened instead of taking part in the conversation was the first sign the date was going south.

Red flag: He ended the date.

Interpretation: He was not very interested. Men don't end dates with women they want to see again. In fact, they will usually do anything they can to prolong the evening, such as suggest after-dinner drinks or a walk.

Red flag: He started to walk toward his apartment.

Interpretation: He wanted to escape first. Men who are interested in women want to make sure they get home safely so that they can see the woman again! They don't scurry back to their own place and hope, as an afterthought, their date gets home safely. And interested men never jump into their cars and peel out of the parking lot while you are still walking to your own car, fiddling with your keys, trying to remember where you parked.

The woman really didn't do anything wrong. All she did was look forward to her date and enjoy the evening. This is why it's extremely important to understand that there are certain players on the field in the game of love, and they can disguise themselves very well. From the "Amateur Player" to the "Player That's Not Playin'," if you are out there dating, it's critical that you know who is on the opposing team!

• • • • • • • • • PLAYERS ON THE FIELD • • • • • • • • •

The guy you met on "The First Date" is one of the many players on the field. He was relatively smooth, seemed easygoing, and said all of the right things. He showed up (which is hard enough for some guys), listened to his date talk, and even parted with the words that so many girls wait all night to hear: "I'll give you a call." Let's pretend you find yourself in the same scenario.

You go on a first date with a guy. You like him, but how do you know if he's the right guy for you? How do you know he's not a serial dater, a no-commitment 'fraidy-cat, or someone you simply don't want calling you?

As a dating coach, I often work just as hard to keep women away from the wrong men as I do trying to find them Mr. Right. By nature, women are givers and nurturers and, as a result, are often more willing to make sacrifices and accept the unacceptable to fix a doomed relationship. Save yourself time and heartache, and don't let that happen to you. The following is a little cheat sheet to help you identify the kind of player you're up against.

Guy #1: The Amateur Player

This guy is trying to have sex with you; the clues are obvious. Read on.

✦ **The day:** The first date is on a Monday, Tuesday, or Wednesday. These nights are unimportant to men, so for them to invest a little time trying to have a one-night stand isn't a big deal. A guy can always TiVo the game or meet up with his friends another night.

✦ **The effort:** Remember, guys are generally lazy; therefore, if he doesn't think you are something superspecial, he will make his attempt to sleep with you as painless as possible. This means he will choose a time and a place that totally suits him. You will most likely be meeting him close to where he lives, and the date will take place at least two hours after he finishes work so that he has time to work out, check scores on ESPN, and walk around his apartment talking to one of his dumb friends on the phone about nothing.

✦ **The place:** He will choose a place that is extremely casual, neighborhood-like, and cheap. He will be waiting for you there, and he will have already had a couple of beers. When you arrive, the Amateur Player will give you "the wave" to come over and pony up to the bar. He will not be waiting outside to greet you like a gentleman.

✦ **His appearance:** He will be clean, but that's about it. This is the guy who puts limited effort into his appearance. He will be dressed for comfort, not style.

✦ **His motive:** He will try to pour as much liquor down your throat as possible. This means he will appear to be "a gentleman" by ordering you a drink or two or three or four. Because the average guy is far less intelligent than the average woman, he will need you in an inebriated state so that you will find his remedial humor cute. He will also want to make sure that you cannot identify his weak and feeble attempts at making you just another one-night stand.

✦ **His MANeuver:** He will get "hands-on" and start pawing at you after you have finished your second drink, or forty-five minutes into the date, whichever comes first. Guys tend to become impatient when their "other brains" are in full control.

✦ **His power move:** After you have been sufficiently "tuned up"—meaning buzzed, tipsy, or a little drunk—he'll start talking about how his place is right around the corner and how he would love your opinion on some rug or plant he just bought. If you don't take his pathetic bait and you remain in the bar, then I can promise you that he will all of a sudden realize that it is starting to get late; he will remember he has an "early start" tomorrow and needs to get to bed early. The Amateur Player is not savvy enough to be subtle. His power move is abrupt and obvious. Once this guy knows he's not getting anywhere with you, he is getting away from you!

In summary, the Amateur Player is young in age or maturity level and rough around the edges. His looks are the main weapon in his arsenal of seduction. His moves are obvious and weak. He is at a point in his life where girls are a sport, and all he is interested in is scoring. No matter what he tells you, the thought of a serious relationship is harder to comprehend than a foreign language. If you are comfortable being a one-night stand, then more power to you. But be aware that when you are doing "the walk of shame" home from his apartment the next morning (he won't be paying for your cab), if he hasn't already forgotten your name, it has been replaced by a number. Yes, men do count how many women they have slept with. I don't know why we do it, we just do. The Amateur Player actually considers intelligence, personality, and conversational ability overrated when it comes to getting a woman into bed. He likes them dumb, easy, and completely unchallenging. His type of woman is more like a blow-up doll with a limited vocabulary—think Coco the famous sign language chimp.

Rules for Dealing with an Amateur, if You Must

Rule #1: If you date an Amateur Player, you must learn to compartmentalize. Identify the scope of the relationship, and take from it what it has to offer. For example, if your career and friends take up 90 percent of your time, then having a purely sexually satisfying relationship might suit your lifestyle. There is nothing wrong with that. You are not a sleaze, a whore, or easy. You are an intelligent woman who has the ability to fulfill her own sexual needs. Be advised if you choose this route, there is no turning back. And expect nothing. If you are at a place in your life where you truly desire a successful relationship, please do not look toward this type of guy to fulfill your needs. You will never be the "X-Factor Girl" who makes him only want to sleep with one woman, exert tons of effort into a relationship, and forget about his friends and freewheeling lifestyle. You could ask for nothing from him, be at his beck and call twenty-four hours a day, and fulfill his every fantasy in the bedroom, and he still won't call back. At this time in his life, he does not have the emotional tools to have a successful relationship.

Rule #2: There are no more dates with this guy after the first one-night stand.

Rule #3: There are only late-night drinks, 2:00 A.M. booty calls, and preplanned quickies.

Rule #4: Only have contact with him once a week for the above-mentioned sexual matters.

Rule #5: No spooning, only limited passionate kissing on the lips, and definitely no staring into his baby blues.

Rule #6: Never, ever, ever spend the night.

Rule #7: No deep personal conversation revealing your emotional needs, your future goals, or descriptions of your soul mate.

Guy #2: The True Professional

This guy is also trying to get into your pants, but you will never suspect it.

✦ **The day:** Your date will most likely be on a Friday or Saturday night. He has to be precise in his attempt to totally misrepresent his intentions.

✦ **The effort:** Everything he does, from the way he asks you out to the car he sends for you to the place he chooses for dinner, will be for effect. But if you think that you could hang out with him for the lifestyle he leads, be aware the most you will get from him are the dinners and the hotel rooms. He is extremely selfish, and in the end he will be cheap. The only cash he will spend is on himself.

✦ **The place:** Unlike the Amateur Player, the True Professional's game is finely tuned. It is hard to identify and truly elaborate. He will go to extreme measures to look the part. He is a showman with no soul or depth. The first date with this master manipulator will be dinner. Coffee or drinks do not provide enough of a stage for him to perform. He needs you to see him as sort of a godfather type. The maître d' will fawn over him almost to the point of kissing his pinky ring (that stuff about the pinky ring was for effect; if he does have a pinky ring . . . RUN!), whisking both of you away from the line at the front of the restaurant and immediately to a table. He will make sure you see him do that macho, cash exchange, departing handshake thing with the maître d' as he leaves. He will be accommodating in a completely controlling way. This means that he will decide what you'll be drinking for a cocktail, and he will choose the wine and your meal. Don't be misled; this might appear chivalrous on the surface, but that is not his intention. He is setting the tone of the relationship, and his melody is complete control.

✦ **His appearance:** He is a master at using props to assist him in creating the perfect story line. These props include such labels as Patek Philippe, Bentley, and Gucci. This man is an egomaniac. His intentions are to impress three categories of people: you, everyone around you, and, most importantly, himself. He is going to hit you with his best right up front. And his "best" consists of material objects because he has no soul of his own.

✦ **His motive:** To paint a fantasy picture of male perfection using such accoutrements as chivalrous acts, renowned restaurants, material objects, and loads of special attention to create a smoke screen that blurs your judgment enough for you to let down your guard and sleep with him.

✦ **His MANeuver:** When you are with him, he will try to make you feel as though you are the only woman in the world. Be aware, he will do this with a combination of compliments that address not only your appearance but also your intellect and personality. They will be delivered effortlessly and with perfect timing to ensure the illusion of sincerity and authenticity.

✦ **His power move:** Please remember everything this guy does is premeditated, from the surface questions he asks about you—so you will genuinely believe he cares—to the incredibly smooth way he redirects each conversation back to himself. He will also throw his patented "dessert move" at you during your first date. Allow me to prepare you for this elaborate move. He will have preordered some dramatically sexy dessert, such as chocolate soufflé, that takes a good twenty minutes to prepare. After the main course is removed and the dessert wine has arrived, he will proceed to change his dinner seating position and cozy up right alongside you. He will raise his glass and make an after-dinner toast that has a heavy sexual undertone. This will be followed by an attempt to feed you the chocolate soufflé in between soft cheek and neck kisses.

In summary, this guy will temporarily walk the walk for you to believe that he is extremely interested in you. He is a sprint player; he comes at you hard and fast with everything he has to completely mislead you into believing he is your dream guy. But, the True Professional does not have the ability or interest in keeping up the pace of being Mr. Wonderful. He is a chameleon who can become anyone for a short period of time just to get you into bed.

Rules for Dealing with the True Professional

Rule #1: Do not take anything this man says to heart. Remember he has said the same things to every girl before you. He uses words as crutches, weapons, and manipulation techniques to get you into his bed.

Rule #2: Don't practice saying your name with his last name, decide how many children you want, or try to figure out if you should reserve matching Eddie Bauer SUVs. There is absolutely no future with this guy. If you have to see him to pass time, which is a mistake anyway, live in the moment and take all the material things he has to offer, such as great dinners and minivacations, with a grain of salt.

Rule #3: Please be sure that you are careful with this guy. He is seeing multiple women along with you. If you decide to sleep with him, you should take the necessary precautions.

Guy #3: The Iceberg Guy

What lies below the surface of this guy is much more appealing than what you actually see.

✦ **The day:** This nonplayer tends to initially use standard dating protocol when he first asks you out. He is a little stiff in the beginning, but his rigidness comes off as formal and respectful, so it tends to be kind of cute. He will ask you out on a Friday or Saturday night.

✦ **The effort:** He will put a lot of effort and thought into your first date. What's interesting is that you will have no idea about the lengths he has gone to in attempting to plan the perfect first date. He will have listened to everything that you said regarding food you like or activities you enjoy.  The date will be preplanned down to the minutest detail, but he'll keep the effort he's made to himself. He is truly secure and doesn't need your compliments regarding his efforts to create a wonderful evening.

✦ **The place:** The locale of the date will most likely be somewhere you had casually mentioned to him when you first met him. It might be a cool restaurant you had said you wanted to try or your favorite coffee shop that you mentioned in passing. Bottom line: this guy listens and is considerate, two extremely important traits.

✦ **His appearance:** This guy is neat and squeaky clean. He will show up in something that is conservative yet trendy. Deep down inside, though, he wants to be cutting edge and is just waiting for a partner in crime to push him to be the trailblazer he is.

✦ **His motive:** The Iceberg Guy is a straight shooter. His motive is to find a special person whom he feels is worth his time. If he has asked you out, he thinks extremely highly of you. He is *not* a one-night-stand guy! Nor is he a serial dater. He picks and chooses cautiously. Do not make the mistake of chalking him up as a geek or an uptight nerd. He is a wild man at heart and just needs a little time to get to know the right girl. He'll then unleash his true personality and transform into every girl's fantasy.

✦ **His MANeuver:** At the end of the date he will give you the most adorable and respectful kiss on the cheek with absolutely no premeditated plan to try to sleep with you.

✦ **His power move:** Because this guy is initially conservative, his big power move will be to extend the date beyond all the preplanned activities and improvise. At this point, you have scored big, and he feels comfortable enough to freewheel and just hang out with you. This is where you'll catch a glimpse of his exciting and spontaneous guy potential.

In summary, the Iceberg Guy is a keeper! He may seem a little stiff at first, but his rigidness is a great character sign that tells you he has evolved way beyond allowing his impulses to control his actions. He operates from the vantage point of focused, logical thought processes and never allows testosterone to rule him. He is worth a second date and further consideration. Each date will bring more excitement. He also takes a while to show you his best.

Rules for Dealing with the Iceberg Guy

Rule #1: Be patient. Allow this guy to unveil himself slowly and show you what lies beneath his surface.

Rule #2: This guy moves at an incredibly slow pace when it comes to emotional intimacy, so never ask him to label your relationship.

Rule #3: Be passive and feminine around him; allow him to take the lead. He needs to feel that you value his honest charm.

Guy #4: The Player Who's Not Playin'

Is this guy for real? Yep.

✦ **The day:** He's not concerned with what day it is, he just wants to go out with you. This guy plays by his own rules and is true to what he feels. If it's Monday and it works for both of you, the date will be Monday. The same goes for Saturday, Sunday, or Thursday. He just wants to see you.

✦ **The effort:** He will do whatever it takes to get you to see him. Nothing is premeditated; it's natural and laid-back. He is accommodating because he doesn't care if he is making more of an effort than you. He doesn't keep score.

✦ **The place:** This guy enjoys having a good time. Because of his security level, he knows he can give you the best date of your life sipping hot chocolate on a Saturday afternoon in the middle of February or at a five-star restaurant on a Saturday night. Location is not important.

✦ **His appearance:** This guy loves to look great. He enjoys life and will look his best whether he's playing paintball or meeting your parents. He likes female attention but is very respectful on dates. He is focused on whom he is with, and no one can take him out of that zone, not even Jessica Biel.

✦ **His motive:** This gentleman has one motive: to genuinely get to know you. He does not play games. He is authentic.

✦ **His MANeuver:** This guy's big maneuver is his spontaneity. He thrives on his ability to be creative, exciting, and extremely entertaining. He has no boundaries and is up for anything. He uses his unpredictability as his charm. A helicopter ride across the Hudson River or an overnight trip to Vegas is always one step away from actually happening when you are with him.

✦ **His power move:** Something completely unexpected. When he falls for you, the most important thing to him will be to make sure he is like no other guy you have ever dated. He will separate himself from the others by his unpredictable surprises and great sense of humor that will always keep you on your toes and wondering what will be next.

In summary, do not, and I repeat, do not fall into the Too-Good-to-Be-True Syndrome. Allow me to explain. Too-Good-to-Be-True Syndrome is when a woman does not believe that the guy she is dating is really who he says he is. She believes that his great behavior, sexy charm, and perfect gentlemanly ways are short-lived stage acts that only an Academy Award–winning actor or the ultimate player could ever be capable of pulling off. Her skepticism is most likely the result of being thoroughly misled and let down in the past by selfish, weak guys whom she had once trusted. It's cool to learn your lesson and be on high alert, but it's another thing to allow yourself to become jaded to the point of completely shutting down. Do not make the mistake of allowing losers who let you down in the past dictate the degree to which you open your heart to future great guys. Please also remember, a lot of successful relationships are the result of great timing. Maybe once he was a horrific player. Maybe once all of his charming actions, sexy rhetoric, and showmanship were only done to bed unsuspecting, naïve women. But maybe, just maybe, he has learned his lessons from all of the hurt he has caused and the loss he has experienced. Maybe the time has come in his life when he uses all of his charm, personality, and sex appeal for all of the right reasons . . . like finding a woman he can truly give himself to forever.

Rule for Dealing with the Player Who's Not Playin' (There's Only One!)

Rule #1: Throw the skepticism aside, drop the jaded behavior, and use trust, courage, and faith to drink this guy in and enjoy everything he has to offer.

Guy #5: The Married Man

There are actually five players on the field, but the fifth one deserves a special category all to himself. Don't get me wrong, it's not because he is so special. It's because he can be very complex, and we want to make sure you are aware of his professional moves. He is the Married Man, and Mr. Betrothed must not be taken lightly. He is smooth and seasoned, and he must be avoided at all costs. He is a serious time waster, and if you are hoping to get a ring of your own one day, take heed: it will most likely not be coming from him. The Married Man ventures outside of his marriage and onto the playing field for a few different reasons:

✦ **He is insecure, and he seeks the attention of many women.** The problem is you will never really know if your attention is enough for him. Let's pretend Mr. Betrothed leaves his wife for you. Then what? Will he finally be satisfied? Will he stop needing extra female attention? Or will you spend the rest of your days wondering if he is cheating on you like he cheated on his wife?

✦ **He is truly unhappy with his marriage but afraid to leave.**
If a man is afraid to leave his wife, then he will always be afraid.
And if you finally persuade him to get the big D (divorce), rest
assured he may wind up being resentful in the long run.

✦ **He can't leave because of the kids or financial reasons, or
so he says.** One out of every two marriages ends in divorce,
and plenty of those marriages have produced children. What
makes his kids so different that they would not be able to handle a divorce? It sounds harsh, but you need to take this statement very seriously because it is simply an excuse for him to
have his cake and eat it too. And if finances are the only reason
that he claims he is not leaving his wife, then he doesn't want
to leave badly enough. My father once told me it's better to be
lonely alone than lonely with someone. If Mr. Betrothed would
rather be lonely in his marriage just so he doesn't have to
struggle financially, then let him be. The Married Man must be
benched the minute you meet him. He will have great moves,
he is quick and skilled, but to save you heartache down the
road, avoid him at every turn.

In summary, just say "I don't" to this guy. He has a serious
case of "ring" worm, and you should avoid him at all costs.
Enough said.

Ladies, take all that you have learned in this chapter to
heart. We want to make sure that you are always aware of how
a man thinks, how he behaves, and most important, what his
intentions are. He can be the hottest guy in the world with

A FEW MORE SECRETS OF THE BOYS CLUB

✦ **Men love a woman with her own identity:** You were an individual without him, so make sure you're an individual with him. Nothing is more attractive than a woman who makes sure a man knows she would be just fine without him.

✦ **Confidence is a turn-on:** There is no other way to be! You must maintain confidence in the way you look, in his feelings toward you, and in all of your actions. A woman who knows she looks great is truly sexy. Look your best always.

✦ **Girls don't call boys:** Guess what, your mama was right! Girls don't call boys. In the beginning, you must make him believe that he is an afterthought. It may sound harsh, old-fashioned, or over-the-top, but until you are dating him and no one else, there is no reason for you to initiate a phone call. If he is thinking about you, he will call.

✦ **Men do not know what they want:** Most of men's actions are driven by impulse, so if they get what they want too soon, they lose interest. If they don't get what they want immediately, it becomes a challenge. Make a man wait! If you give yourself to him on the first date, there will be no second.

✦ **The male species is the most easily intimidated species on the planet:** Your successes, female strength, and intellect can be liabilities with the wrong guy because he will be scared of you. You must find a man who embraces who you

> are and what you do. If you don't, you will be compromising forever.
>
> ✦ **Complete availability is a turnoff:** Make yourself unavailable, even if you have the whole weekend free! Never say "YES!" the first time he asks you for a date unless he asks you out three days in advance. Let him understand that you have a life, and you are fitting him in. Just trust us on this one!

the greatest lines ever, but if he is not ready for a relationship because of where he is in his life, or his only intention is to pass the time with you, or worse, sleep with you for sport, you need to know sooner rather than later. You can poll your friends, ask his buddies, and even become close with his mom, but if a guy is not interested in you, nothing will make him pick up that phone to call. Arm yourself with the Secrets of the Boys Club, and you'll never have to wonder whether or not there will be a second date.

THE BOND GIRL

She's the girl that every woman wants to be.

She instantly grabs the attention of any man, any-time, anywhere.

She's sexy, sleek, smooth, and well put together.

She's the Bond Girl; the girl that James Bond chases, loves, and will risk life and limb to be with. And she's not just eye candy; she plays a critical role in every mission James Bond takes on. Often, she's the one that has to swoop in and rescue J.B. when he's in danger. In the end, she's always the girl he chooses. The truth is every guy wants to be with a Bond Girl.

But take heart: the Bond Girl isn't always a size 4, and she doesn't always have perfectly coiffed hair. However, men are visual creatures, and, like it or not, the initial thing most men notice about a woman is her appearance. The good news is you have more control over the way you look than you may think. It's not all that difficult to turn a guy on and pull him into your web with a few smart makeup, hair, and clothing choices. So, how do you become a Bond Girl? In this chapter, we'll show you how to make the transformation. First, I'll map out the Bond Girl's physical attributes. Then, Tamsen and I will give you pointers on how to act and look the part.

•••• THE TOTAL BOND GIRL PACKAGE ••••

All women are capable of creating the Bond Girl look by enhancing the four most important features that men first notice in women. Here is the breakdown of how a guy checks you out when you pass him on the street: As you approach him, he isn't homing in on your Jimmy Choo shoes; he first notices your shoulder, breast, and waist proportions, with the focus being on your boobs. He will then look at (in this exact order) your lips, eyes, hair length, and then finally your full face. As you pass him, if you have piqued his interest just enough, he will stop in his tracks and do a full 180-degree turn so he can blatantly zero in on your rear end. Bottom line (pardon the pun), all of your accessories, expensive clothes, and cool new handbags take a backseat (sorry, couldn't resist) to the previously mentioned male-centric viewing pleasures.

To break it down even further, I've come up with a detailed list of what men want to see in a woman; put it all together, and you have yourself one smokin' hot Bond Girl. Warning: at first blush, this list might seem superficial, but ladies, hear me out; I'm simply relaying to you what men tell me. I know because I ask them. Each time I sit down with one of my male clients, I question him about what he wants in a woman, and this list is the gist of what the guys have told me:

✦ **A proportionate body that is womanly:** Men don't want to be with women who are built like teenage boys. We love curves. Think Scarlett Johansson, Elizabeth Hurley, and Catherine Zeta-Jones.

✦ **Sensual lips:** A lot of male fantasies stem from this body part. In our eyes, you can't be too rich, have too many diamonds, or have lips that are too large.

✦ **Cleopatra eyes:** Men love huge, sexy eyes.

✦ **Long, silky hair:** Men equate long hair with femininity. For some reason men have this fantasy of sniffing your hair, letting it fall down onto their faces, or grabbing a handful in the heat of the moment.

• • • • • • • • • THE BOND GIRL 'TUDE • • • • • • • • •

 "Dress shabbily, they notice the dress. Dress impeccably and they remember the woman." This observation from fashion legend and former Bond Girl Coco Chanel describes a theory I embrace when providing image consulting for our female clients.

At this point, I know what you are probably thinking: "Tamsen, I spend all day getting ready for a date. I can't do any more than that." Or "I don't want to be with a guy who is only worried about how I look." The truth is this is not about your date or about him; this is about how you are dressing, feeling, and portraying yourself to the world for *your* life and *yourself*!

When it comes to preparing for a date, believe me, I've been there. I've spent all day getting ready for a date that turned out to be a flop. Here's a list of my predate preps:

TO DO:

8:00 A.M.:	Hit the gym (had pizza the night before)
10:00 A.M.:	Nails (manicure/pedicure)
11:30 A.M.:	Wax (all essential body parts)
12:30 P.M.:	Hit the mall to buy new outfit
3:00 P.M.:	Leave mall, exhausted, annoyed, and $150 in the hole
4:00 P.M.:	Lay out two new outfits I can't afford and decide between them
5:00 P.M.:	Hit the shower
6:00 P.M.:	Fix hair and makeup while dancing to Madonna, Cher, or Destiny's Child
8:00 P.M.:	Date begins
11:00 P.M.:	Commence waiting for him to call for second date

The good news is once you start your life as a Bond Girl, the all-day date preparations become completely unnecessary. The Bond Girl is always at her best. She goes through life ready at any time to rendezvous with James Bond, and she knows that first and foremost, looking good is about having the right attitude as opposed to the perfect pair of wedges.

• • • • • • • BOND GIRL FASHION TIPS • • • • • • •

Ladies, if you want to be attractive to the opposite sex, you have to do the work. Forget the term "natural beauty"; there's no such thing. Every woman has to put effort into her appearance. And full-blown Bond Girls have a beauty regimen that's guaranteed to make you look your most fabulous. Read on.

Clothes

Less is more. This doesn't mean less clothing; it means simple is sexy. First, let's consider the colors you are choosing. Every woman has a sense of which colors she looks best in, which ones best complement her eyes and skin tone. But in case you're ever unsure, remember black is universally flattering, hence the popularity of the classic little black dress.

For a casual drink or dinner, it may be just the thing to wear. Darker shades tend to create a slimming look on women and, in fact, can make you look up to five pounds lighter in some cases. But be careful not to dress your little black number up to the nines. You don't want to overdo it. Whichever color you choose, avoid stripes in either direction unless you are trying to add five pounds to your frame. Vertical can be just as bad as horizontal.

Next, if you have a large chest, try to avoid white shirts. I have this problem and have all but eliminated white oxford shirts from my wardrobe. They look great on thin women, but if you are curvy they tend to overaccentuate your positives.

Finally, make sure you are fitted with the right bra.

Jeans can be another fashion faux pas if you are not wearing the right size. If you have to jump up and down to get them on, lie on the bed to pull them up, or solicit help from your roommate, it's time to go shopping for a new pair. Make sure your clothes fit. In this instance, size matters. Clothes that are too tight or too loose can make you look like you are overweight. The goal is to look proportionate, pretty, and put together, not pudgy.

Most important, when it comes to dressing for a date, be comfortable with what you're wearing. Don't dress like someone you're not. It's tough to keep up an act, so it's best not to start with one. And dress appropriately for the date location: jeans and a T-shirt may not be right for dinner at the hottest restaurant in town. That little black dress and heels might be just the thing.

Shoes

I know, I know. I love my Birkenstocks too! But if you're looking to turn a guy's head, you need to add heels and strappy sandals to your dating wardrobe. Shoes play an important part in your overall presentation, even if they are the last things he looks at. Here are a few shoe tips:

+ If you are a larger woman, dainty shoes can look out of proportion.
+ If you are on the shorter side, a great pair of *comfortable* heels will elongate your legs and give them a sexy shape.
+ During the summer, men love high-heeled sandals so they can see your toes! (A pedicure is a must.)
+ If it's winter, pick the high-heeled black boot of your choice and head out for a night on the town.
+ Try not to exceed three inches, unless you are a pro walking in high heels. You don't want to spill out on the floor as you try to make your way to the bar. Plus, if you're hobbling into your date making funny faces because your shoes are cutting off your circulation, you will look pained and tortured instead of confident and sexy.

Accessories

Lose the distracting jewelry—you want to hypnotize him with your amazing eyes, not with an oversized swinging pendant or chandelier earrings that reach your shoulders and play a symphony every time you move your head. Again, less is more. It's wonderful that you have huge diamonds and lots of trendy bangles, but keep them at home; otherwise, you run the risk of coming across as tacky and reminding him of his wacky Aunt Ethel.

BOND GIRL BEAUTY TIPS

Each of us is born with the physical characteristics that our parents' gene combo gave us. But in this day and age, there's no excuse for not accentuating your positives and camouflaging or getting rid of your negatives. When it comes to looking your most beautiful, embrace makeup and the litany of other fantastic beauty products on the market. With a little research and effort on your part, you can have come-hither eyes; soft, creamy skin; and a sparkling smile—all attributes men are looking for in a Bond Girl. Read on for the specifics.

Eyes

It's all in the eyes. I believe they tell a lot, if not everything, about a person. Men believe they tell them how good a woman will be in bed. You've heard the saying "bedroom eyes." Well, now I'm going to tell you how to get those bedroom eyes. First, make sure you are wearing concealer, and make sure it's not caked on. Concealer will eliminate any dark under-eye circles, and it adds brightness to your face. When your eyes pop, you instantly look younger, not over the hill and exhausted. However, nothing is worse than concealer that cracks under your eyes every time you crack a smile. So, use it in moderation, but make sure you use it.

Next, go easy on the eye shadow. Yes, the models on the runway are often done up with dramatic blues and pinks, but this rock-star look doesn't translate when you're sitting at dinner under fluorescent lighting. Giving yourself some definition on the crease of your eyes is one thing, but looking like a clown is quite another. I prefer natural colors because they seem to work for almost everyone and can be used year-round.

Now, the best for lash! A few false eyelashes will do wonders for your eyes. (You can pick them up at any drugstore for less than three dollars a box.) This TV trick definitely translates to real life. Ever wonder how reporters and news anchors look so wide awake even though you saw them twelve hours earlier covering the same election or hurricane? Well, false eyelashes are definitely an industry standard. Just add about four to six lashes to the outer corners of your lash line for each eye, and you will instantly give yourself an ultrasexy look. The lashes open up your eyes and in the process make you look younger and brighter.

Hair

Next up, hair. As Matt mentioned, long, silky hair is definitely a turn-on to men. If you've got it, flaunt it. But don't try to keep up with the hair color of the week. If you are a better brunette, don't go blonde. And if you are a natural blonde, stay true to your roots. Hair color and highlights are here to complement your look, not to overpower it. One color you shouldn't be natural about: gray. If you have any grays peeking out of your mane, get thee to a salon! Also, be sure to trim your hair regularly; there's no excuse for looking shaggy. It's a good idea to trim your hair every six weeks to make sure there are no damaged or split ends.

Skin

Makeup is fine, but if you are caking it on to cover up problem skin, you need to think again. In some cases, I have found that too much makeup, improperly applied, can actually add years to the face. This is probably the last thing any of us wants to do, so you should try to keep your makeup as natural as possible. After all, when the time comes for you to sleep over, you want him to recognize you when you wake up in the morning. Also, if you are having skin problems, take a trip to a top dermatologist in your area. Take my word for it; there are several very successful treatment options for whatever skin issue is getting you down. And be sure to invest in high-quality makeup. Ask your dermatologist which brands of makeup and moisturizer she recommends for your complexion.

Lips

Neutral lip gloss over your favorite color gives your mouth that important kissability factor and gives thinner lips a more alluring, plump appearance. Over-the-counter lip plumpers, which cost less than fifteen dollars at most makeup stores, are another inexpensive way to give your lips a pouty presence! Lip plumpers work by temporarily irritating lips and causing them to swell slightly.

Teeth

White, beautiful teeth are a must. This means if you are a coffee drinker, are a smoker, or just haven't paid a lot of attention to your pearly whites, there is no better time than the present to whiten up your chops. And there's no need to spend a ton of money on expensive bleaching treatments. Instead, a number of companies have created teeth-whitening kits, which will run you only about thirty dollars. It's worth every penny.

· · · · · · · · · · THE BOND GIRL BODY · · · · · · · · · ·

You don't have to train for a year to have a hot Bond Girl body. I've spent fifteen years in the fitness industry, and I'll fill you in on some very simple exercises that you can do to transform your body in a very short amount of time. The combination of focused daily fitness training and a healthy eating plan will give you the fastest results.

Diet

Can I tell you how much I hate the word *diet*? Did you know that 85 percent of people who go on diets fail to lose weight! Does this tell you something? THEY DON'T WORK! So instead of telling you to eat some ridiculous-tasting, low-calorie piece of chemical, I am going to tell you four things you can do to shed pounds.

✦ **Create a food diary.** Write down the time and content of everything you eat on a daily basis for a week. This will make you conscious of just how much you eat every day. When you see it written down in black and white, you will clearly understand why you are not at your goal weight.

✦ **Cut out all bread, pasta, and rice for two weeks.** This will be extremely difficult because our society is addicted to carbohydrates. But if you can do this successfully for the full two weeks, I guarantee that you'll drop pounds.

✦ **Load up on your greens.** Vegetables are a great source of carbohydrates. You really cannot eat enough of them. As they are made up of about 80 percent water, they won't add many calories to your diet. Just don't load them with butter and olive oil. My personal favorites are spinach, broccoli, green peppers, and asparagus.

✦ **Reduce the size of your meals throughout the day.** Make your largest meal breakfast, followed by a medium-sized lunch and a small dinner, and never eat after 8:30 P.M. That's when your metabolism is running at its slowest pace.

The Titus Tush

A shapely rear end will stop all male traffic. When men see a round, tight, perfectly shaped tush, they temporarily lose control and act on pure instinct. The male mind is completely visual, and during this moment of intense sexual desire, all men are ripe for the picking. So the next logical question is, "How do I get a world-class ass?" The following exercises and nutrition tips will give you a step up when it comes to cultivating your rear.

STAIRS. I love what staircase interval training does for a woman's rear end. It can be done at home or at the gym. Stair training is great because it actually is high-rep, light–weight resistance training, the kind of exercise that helps shape, tighten, and create lean muscle mass. Think about it: you are lifting your body weight each time you step up a stair during your ascension. You do this multiple times during a staircase workout. Additionally, the actual movement of the body when climbing a stairs will shape your thighs, lift and harden your butt, and give you a flat, hard stomach. On top of all that, staircase interval training will give you fantastic calf muscles in heels. Even more important, you will burn the most fat in the shortest period of time.

Remember, you are lifting your body weight against gravity whenever you step up onto the next stair. This is much more difficult than walking horizontally and burns about twice as much fat as other kinds of exercise.

You can use a StairMaster at the gym, or you can find a staircase in your apartment building, in your home, in your office, or outside with at least ten steps per flight. In the gym, start using the StairMaster for thirty minutes, three days a week. The goal is to work up to an hour a day, three days a week. If you are doing this exer-cise at home, try to start with two flights of stairs. The best staircases are straight with mul-tiple flights. Next, run up the two flights of steps (skip-ping a step) five times. Accelerate through the first landing right into the next flight of steps. When you reach the landing after the sec-ond flight of steps, stop and do fifteen squats. Do the squats each time you reach the top of the second flight. Do not touch the railings on the way up the staircases. On the way down, use each step, and bring your knees up higher than you nor-mally would. Feel free to use the railing for balance on the way down.

LUNGES. As far as I'm concerned, lunges should be a daily staple for all women starting at the age of sixteen. Talk about an exercise that can create a heavenly bum! Lunges are equivalent to the plastic surgeon's knife. This exercise will re-create your lower body and, when done correctly and consistently, will give you shapely thighs, rock-hard hamstrings, and a round, high rear end.

Start with your feet shoulder width apart. Then, take your right foot and step forward. When you are stepping forward, your upper body and your right knee should not fall forward. Make sure your knee is at a ninety-degree angle, just over your toes; you can really hurt yourself if you do these wrong. Keeping your body upright, dip your knee close to the ground (without touching it) and then return to the starting position. Repeat ten times on the right leg, then switch and do the same using your left leg. Shoot for a goal of four sets of lunges with ten repetitions each.

Bond Girl Breasts

Breasts play an important role in drawing male attention. In fact, men look at boobs first. And it's not all about size. Men would much rather see smaller, well-shaped breasts than huge, sloppy ones. Breast fitness is a very important part of keeping your body in shape and desirable to men. It starts with wearing a bra that fits properly and gives you adequate support. This is not just important for looking great in clothes and enhancing your natural shape. It also will help keep the muscles that help fight gravity taut, which will keep your chest perky and firm. When exercising, be sure to wear a sports bra that keeps your breasts steady. To look fabulous in clothes, and for extra cleavage, wear a wire push-up bra. These days many bra manufacturers sell wire push-up bras that are comfortable and all but invisible under clothes. Last, regular push-ups or knee push-ups ("girl" push-ups) will actually keep your breasts perky.

• • • • • • BOND GIRL INSIDE AND OUT • • • • • •

 Remember, while the package may hook them, it's what's on the inside that'll hold them. The following list of personality traits ensures the Bond Girl is as attractive on the inside as she is on the outside.

The Bond Girl Never Talks About Herself Too Much

She is dating a secret agent, for goodness' sakes, so the biggest part of the Bond Girl's allure is her mysterious nature and the fact that she never, ever reveals herself too soon to anyone. Try not to discuss every single detail about yourself, your last relationship, or the three insane ex-boyfriends. Keep it all under wraps until you're sure he's not a double agent. Seriously, there is nothing worse than talking the fun out of the beginning of a relationship. It's an exciting time for you to slowly get to know one another.

The Bond Girl Never Jumps In Too Fast

Yes, she is adventurous and exciting to be with, but she's never too eager to jump into a relationship too fast. Here's why: early on, most men have a serious fear of commitment. They know that seeing a woman too frequently will lead her to believe he is her boyfriend, and, as a result, he will lose his freedom. Of course, we girls know this is not the case, but that is what men believe. You must respect this, not only for his sake, but also for your own. Besides, can you really know after only three dates that he is "the one"? Maybe, but most likely it will take more time than that. Therefore, don't discuss your future together, don't bring up your best friend's new baby, and don't let him into your life too soon. A Bond Girl lets things progress at a steady pace.

The Bond Girl Never Has Unrealistic Expectations

Every woman gives the same answer when asked what type of guy she is looking for: sexy, tall, and handsome. The problem is that we aren't all Cinderellas, and there are very few available princes. In fact, 99 percent of the time guys will fall way short of your expectations, mainly because you often have impractical expectations. This is not to say that you are supposed to settle, but if you are looking for Prince Charming to sweep you off your feet and ride away with you into the sunset, it's just not going to happen! Besides, the Bond Girl is busy trying to better herself, so passively waiting for a prince is not her style anyway. She'd rather go out for a run or a pedicure.

The Bond Girl Never Loses Her Identity

You meet a guy. You decide he's "the one." Every weekend you go out with his friends, hang in his favorite haunts, and take up watching football just to be with him. That's love . . . right? WRONG! I cannot stress this enough: don't ever lose yourself in a man. Maintain your identity, or you will end up without one. Don't lose your edge. If before you met "the one," you got your nails done every Saturday morning with your friends, keep doing it. You don't need to sit home in case he decides he wants to go to the mall. Or, if you spend the night at his house, don't feel committed to go have breakfast with him. Stick to your schedule. Another example: you love to work out, but he has never seen the inside of a gym. So, you give up your trainer, stop running after work, and go out to eat with him after a hard day at the office. Do this, and you will actually convince him to start running . . . from you. Keep your life when you start dating a guy, and he will keep you. Remember, he chased that hot, independent girl with the sassy and sexy attitude who did her own thing.

The Bond Girl Never Sleeps with Him on the First Date

It's simple: if you want a second date, then stay out of the sack on the first. If you sleep with a man on the first date, he will assume that's how you operate. Don't think you can convince him otherwise by rolling over afterward and saying, "I never do this!" He won't believe you, whether it's true or not. And he probably won't even hear it because he'll be too busy wondering how long he has to stick around and pretend to be interested before he can bolt and not look like a pig. The Bond Girl knows that she will get the guy by the end of the movie, so why would she sleep with him during the first fifteen minutes of the film when there is plenty of time before the credits roll?

The Bond Girl Is Cool, Confident, and Collected

Most men can't get enough of a confident woman who is secure with who she is and what she is feeling. It's not a turn-on when you are emotional, needy, and, worst of all, possessive. Unless your secret agent is undressing a woman with his eyes (or you actually catch him physically removing a woman's clothing), then don't say anything when another beautiful woman walks by. In fact, to throw him completely off guard, acknowledge her, smile, and let him know that you don't consider her a threat. Also, don't be wishy-washy when it comes to making decisions. If he asks you where you want to go eat, tell him. Never say, "Wherever you want to go." You have been picking out restaurants for yourself for much of your adult life—why stop now?

• • • • • BOND GIRL RULES TO LIVE BY • • • • •

Once she's attracted the right man, the Bond Girl knows how to maintain her cool at the beginning of a relationship. Follow these rules to keep your James Bond coming back for more.

Never Utter the "Final Four"

The "final four" are four words that will make almost any man run if they are uttered in the first few months of a relationship. No matter how great you get along, how many friends he has introduced you to, or how often you have slept together, rest assured, your courtship will come to a screeching halt if you mention these four words: *"Where is this going?"* Let him dictate the pace of the relationship; if you don't, you'll instead be asking, "Where did he go?"

Watch Your Language

I'm not talking about curse words (though you should prob-ably try not to shock him with profanity on the first date). We are talking about the words that many men find offensive or at least pretty scary. Let him take the lead when it comes to words like *wedding*, *marriage*, *love*, and *children*. For the time being, take those words out of your vocabulary.

Never Humiliate Him in Front of Friends, Family, or Coworkers

Have you ever been standing between that couple who likes to throw cutting remarks at one another? It's not only uncomfortable for third parties, it's damaging all around. Avoid being those people; be loving and kind, and never try to degrade a man for a cheap laugh. Not only will doing so make you look bad in front of others, but it will also make you look bad in front of him. If you have constructive criticism for him, save it until you are alone together and you can tell him in private.

Once You Become Involved, Say "Yes" to Sex

That's right, the hot sex doesn't stop once you get the guy. Nothing is more frustrating to a man than a woman who is sexual in the beginning and then uses it as a weapon once she's nabbed her guy. Don't play games. On the flip side, don't say "yes" too soon. Doing so can make for a very short-term relationship. Any man is going to try to sleep with you if you are a sexy, attractive woman; it's up to you to keep him at bay until you are ready to say "yes" for the long haul.

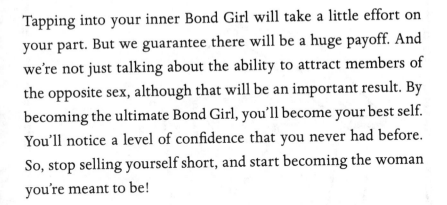

Tapping into your inner Bond Girl will take a little effort on your part. But we guarantee there will be a huge payoff. And we're not just talking about the ability to attract members of the opposite sex, although that will be an important result. By becoming the ultimate Bond Girl, you'll become your best self. You'll notice a level of confidence that you never had before. So, stop selling yourself short, and start becoming the woman you're meant to be!

3

THE LOVE SHACK

Matt and I were sitting in the Four Seasons Hotel in New York City wondering what she was going to look like. On the phone, she had sounded perfect. Her grammar was impeccable, she said all the right things, and she seemed very excited about meeting a great man. Matt and I were convinced we would be sending her out on a date and have her married within six months. When she arrived, we were right on the mark. She was perfect! In fact, I found myself feeling a little bit jealous of her as I wondered how she managed to have it all so together. Miss Manners had a great job, lived in a great neighborhood in Manhattan, and was young, pretty, and perfectly put together. Instantly, we both knew whom her perfect match would be. We'll call him Mr. Manhattan. Mr. Manhattan had been a member of Matt's Little Black Book for about eight months. He was an absolute doll—good-looking, well off, and definitely ready to commit.

After getting all of Miss Manners's information and meeting with her a few more times, Matt made the introduction. We couldn't wait to hear from Mr. Manhattan after the first date. We just knew he would be smitten. But the phone call we got the next day was not only alarming but downright frightening.

According to Mr. Manhattan, they went to dinner and had a great time; they even went out for drinks afterward to keep the night going. He walked her home, and she asked him in for a nightcap. This is something we don't recommend, especially on a first date, but they were getting along great, so it might have ended up OK. I'll let Matt take the story from here.

••••••• LITTLE SHACK OF HORRORS •••••••

Miss Manners's apartment was on the Upper East Side and had a great view of the Chrysler Building. However, my guy didn't get a chance to take in the view because he couldn't tear his eyes away from the rest of the place. Scattered everywhere throughout the apartment were self-help books, including a stack on the back of the toilet. Piles of weight-loss tapes and motivational DVDs lined the living room walls. The couch, where apparently she camped out most nights, had a blanket and pillow on it. And all over the apartment were photographs of her and some guy. It was obvious it wasn't her brother. The "drink" she had invited him up for turned out to be a half-empty bottle of merlot that had a "vinegar-like" smell. Staggering through the place was a mangy-looking cat that had left half of his fur on the blanket on the couch. Mr. Manhattan was polite enough not to discuss any of the smells in the apartment with the two of us.

Alarmed and embarrassed, Tamsen and I met with Miss Manners to find out what was up. Was it a bad week? Was she too busy at work to clean? Was it her brother's apartment? Miss Manners looked surprised at our round of questioning and said, "No, that's my apartment. I sleep on the couch when I've had too much to drink, and my motivational books get me through each week. Plus, I'm so busy, I don't really have time to clean." To which I replied, "Miss Manners, you have got to make time. When a man walks into your home, he pictures himself there; all poor Mr. Manhattan could picture was his escape!" It was then that Matt and I realized that women don't know what a man sees when he crosses their threshold. We decided right then and there to launch a dating program that focuses on women's houses and explains what men think when they enter "the bachelorette pad." This chapter will give you the rundown of the info we share with our clients in that program.

WHAT IS THE LOVE SHACK?

When I was a child, each night I crawled under a white eyelet duvet on my canopy bed and went to sleep surrounded by my stuffed animal collection. As a little girl, your chamber is all decorated for you, the princess, who is just waiting for your prince to come along to take you on over to his castle. But your prince never climbed through your window to whisk you down the wall of your tower and rescue you, did he? Instead, like me, you packed up your stuffed animal collection and Judy Blume books, shoved all your belongings into your broken-down car, and drove halfway across the country. You then crammed your belongings, stuffed animal collection and all, into a dorm or studio or small one-bedroom apartment that overlooked a concrete parking lot.

But regardless of where you are in life, you must make your home your own castle. Don't worry, no guy is going to do a white glove inspection, but he will notice details such as your doll collection peering at him when he is trying to make out with you and books with titles like *Why All Men Suck*. Matt and I like to refer to your home as your "Love Shack." As the phrase implies, your home serves as a symbol of how much you love yourself and also . . . well, you can use your imagination for the rest.

WHY IS THE LOVE SHACK IMPORTANT?

The Love Shack: "It's a little old place where we can get together," according to a 1989 song by the B52's. It's also a place men use to judge women to figure out who they really are. If your bachelorette pad has tiger-striped pillows and hot pink rugs, he may go running for the hills, or at least head over to the nearest Pottery Barn to buy you a gift certificate, so you can redecorate. More important, your guy needs to feel comfortable and at ease when he spends time at your place. Men are full of all sorts of anxieties and insecurities that women have no idea about. I am once again going to be a "traitor" to my gender and reveal some of the most surprisingly ridiculous thoughts that go through a guy's mind when he makes his first visit to your place. Come along with me, step into his mind in real time as he prepares to check out your place for the very first time.

Mr. Right Now: *"God, finally I get asked upstairs! She's a lucky girl because if she hadn't invited me to her place this weekend that would have been it! Who am I kidding? God, look at her ass. I might chase that thing forever. Anyway, this is it, dude. It's gonna happen! I hope she has an awesome couch 'cause that's where I'm going to go for it. She mentioned something about a cat—God, I hate cats! Why doesn't she have a dog? They're so much cooler. Now I'm going to have to listen to her fawn over Mr. Puss and Boots. The things I do for sex! I hope there is a way to get her to the couch. . . . Of course there will be; she probably has an awesome TV right in front of it. I wonder if she has anything in there to eat. I hope she's not one of those lollipop-head girls who doesn't eat and only has lettuce and water in the fridge. And I hope she doesn't put me through show-and-tell hour by showing me pictures of relatives and friends that I couldn't care less about. Oh God, now I have to use the bathroom. I hope it's not close to the living room, and I pray there is air freshener in there or at least matches! Speaking of her bathroom, first thing I'm doing is checking out her medicine cabinet to see if she's on any crazy pills or worse—Valtrex! OK, here we go. She's opening the door . . ."*

As Mr. Right Now's thoughts (*thoughts* is a strong word, I know) go through his brain, here's what's going on in Miss Thing's mind:

Miss Thing: *"I think I've played all my cards right so far. The first date was a casual meeting for cocktails. After two drinks and a wonderful hour and a half, I said good night leaving him wanting more. Date number two was dinner. I made sure he picked me up downstairs in the lobby so he couldn't figure out which unit I lived in. The third time I saw him was for brunch followed by an afternoon of Rollerblading. I even managed to resist his adorable attempt to spend the afternoon 'blading in bed' when we had to go back to his place after brunch because he so conveniently forgot his skates. And now: dinner and a movie at my place! OK, let me go through my checklist again: my place is spotless; the movie from Netflix is on the coffee table along with the Chinese, Japanese, Italian, and Thai delivery menus, so we can order in. Am I missing anything?"*

Unfortunately for Miss Thing, she probably did miss a thing or two or three. Ask yourself, what is a man really looking for when he enters your domain? Is he looking at the architecture? The cleanliness? Or does his analysis of your Love Shack go a bit deeper? The answer: As perfect and as sexy as you think you have made your apartment for Mr. Right Now, there's a good chance that you have completely missed taking care of some aspects that will reveal all of your deepest, darkest secrets. Lucky for you, we've prepared a checklist of everything you need to do to prepare your abode.

•••• BOY SLUMBER PARTY CHECKLIST ••••

Take our advice: before you invite him up to your place, make sure you guy-proof your pad so he doesn't go running for the door before he even gains access to your bedroom. Later in this chapter, we'll tell you how to decorate your apartment in a way that a man will love, but here's the quick fix for getting your apartment guy-ready at the last minute:

✦ **Guy-proofing and your door:** Get rid of anything on your front door other than a handle or a door knocker. Please don't tack up cute sayings, macramé art, or holiday ornamentation. Decorative door mats in an apartment can also be alarming.

Reason: Men like simplicity and mystery. A door full of your favorite sayings or decorations reveals everything about you, which quite frankly is a turnoff to most men. Plus, it will remind them of their grandmother's home in the country. This is the last place he wants to think about before gaining entry into your bedroom.

✦ **Guy-proofing and your pet population:** If you have more than one cat, please make sure that you give all the others away, and never admit to having had them. Or at least have a friend watch them for the night.

Reason: There is just way too much of a "spinster" connotation associated with cats in general, and we don't want to give him the wrong idea this early in the game. Let him meet Mr. Meow and his sister during his second visit.

✦ **Guy-proofing and your family photo gallery:** You must take down any framed photographs of your parents, grandparents, or any other authoritative figures that are hanging in your foyer.

Reason: This is way too much for him to handle right when he walks in and will also make him feel like he is being immediately judged as well as watched like a hawk. It sounds crazy, but trust me, I have "face downed" many relatives in their picture frames in women's apartments.

✦ **Guy-proofing and your religious beliefs:** There should be no religious worship symbols on the walls. And remove all religious books such as Bibles, Korans, or Torahs that are prominently displayed on tables or nightstands.

Reason: This is not to say that you cannot be religious to date, but you don't want him to feel uncomfortable by bringing back flashes of Sister Mary and his Holy Communion during his first visit.

✦ **Guy-proofing and your personals:** Keep all closet doors shut. This includes lingerie drawers.

Reason: Your Imelda Marcos shoe collection and your Seven jean infatuation will only make him feel like you are a senseless spendthrift who will be way too expensive for him to keep. Plus, you are a mysterious woman, and he doesn't need to share in all of your secrets as soon as he comes over.

✦ **Guy-proofing and knickknacks:** Be careful with dolls, figurines, or any other collectibles that you have lining your mantel or shelves. They are of no interest to a man and are a serious turnoff.

Reason: Collectibles are another reminder of our mothers, grandmothers, and any other elderly woman who collects knickknacks. Plus, I have found that many men equate these displays with women who have too much time on their hands.

✦ **Guy-proofing and your weight-loss regimen:** Try to be subtle about weight-loss drinks, diet frozen dinners, and energy supplements. And do not have an empty refrigerator; you should make sure you always have some type of solid food in your refrigerator that is visible.

Reason: An empty fridge is not "cool" to a guy. I know that it's something many singles joke about, but to a man who may be serious about you, it's not a laughing matter. Men like to know that you have the ability to care for them. They like to picture coming over for a sexy, Italian dinner and a bottle of wine. And weight-loss drinks and frozen dinners will cool off any thoughts of a hot night in. Men don't want to know that you actually have to work to maintain your figure.

✦ **Guy-proofing and your exes:** Remove any and all pictures of ex-boyfriends, even if you are still friends with them.

Reason: This one should be pretty self-explanatory, but I want to make sure you "get the picture." No guy is interested in seeing your ex-boyfriend staring back at him from your wall. He will immediately compare himself to your ex, and if he pales in comparison (in his mind), you will have little chance of moving forward in a healthy manner with this relationship. That is because one simple picture of Mr. X will bring out feelings of jealousy and insecurity. Plus it signifies that despite the fact that your last relationship has ended, you can't let it go.

✦ **Guy-proofing and roomies:** If you have roommates, please coordinate overnight guests.

Reason: A man doesn't want to sleep at a youth hostel. It's totally fine to have a roommate, but no man wants to bump into another girl or a guy, for that matter, in your bathroom in the middle of the night.

✦ **Guy-proofing and the team:** If you are a sports freak, this will probably earn you points with him, but please take down any banners or posters of your favorite team, and limit sports talk to Sunday afternoons.

Reason: Throwing on a baseball cap and surprising him with tickets to see your favorite team is one thing, but turning into his frat brother before the game by painting your face in the home team's colors while you guzzle beers and scream at the TV is quite another. Remember to always maintain your femininity, even in your own home.

✦ **Guy-proofing and your medicine cabinet:** Do a sweep to make sure your bathroom medicine cabinet is clear of all antifungals, antidepressants, yeast infection creams, and hair removal potions.

Reason: Men actually like to believe that women don't go to the bathroom, never have their periods, or even sweat for that matter. We don't want to picture hair in any undesirable places, and we don't want to know that you become a different person if you skip your meds. Please allow this fantasy to continue.

✦ **Guy-proofing and self-improvement:** All personal items such as diaries, self-help and relationship books (especially your copy of *Why Hasn't He Called?*—no need to give your secrets away!), and weight-loss equipment purchased on late-night infomercials are to be put away along with all of your favorite late-night toys.

Reason: Many men believe self-help books are for the emotionally fragile, and they don't want to see that in a woman they are starting to become interested in. The male ego would also like to believe that women's use of sex toys is only with men and as a mild supplement (not a substitute) to their incredible sexual technique.

✦ **Guy-proofing and self-affirmation:** All female-centric, slightly neurotic, self-affirming, motivational sayings that are affixed to the refrigerator door by butterfly magnets have to be taken down.

Reason: These little sayings make sense to you alone, and he will never understand what your mantra of the moment means. In addition, you don't want him to ask you what "I am woman, hear me roar" really means to you.

✦ **Guy-proofing and your dirty laundry:** Do not leave dirty clothes hanging over the arm of your treadmill or behind the couch.

Reason: Men equate slovenly living conditions with poor feminine hygiene. It's true.

WHAT I SAW IN TAMSEN'S LOVE SHACK

 With all of this discussion regarding what to have and have not in your home to create an atmosphere that men will embrace, I just remembered a little story about Tamsen's apartment that merits telling. When I first met this hot little news chick, I became very interested in getting to know everything about her. At this time Tamsen was completely career focused. In every way, she was devoted to making it to New York as a reporter/anchor and wasn't interested in much else. Because of that, she had her apartment in what I now call "standby, move-out condition." When I first walked in, I was convinced she was either a gypsy or a bag lady.

When we started dating—before I saw her apartment—I only saw the best of Tamsen. To me she was charming, sexy, and superintelligent. I was crazy about her from "hello." But I knew I had to check out where she lived before I could draw the full picture of her. So when I finally got the "stay in for dinner and a movie" invite, I knew it was showtime! When the night came, I polished my shoes, made my hair look real spiffy, and got a cab to her apartment building. I had only made it to the lobby thus far; all the doormen and I were by now on a first-name basis. So when I arrived in the lobby alone with flowers and asked them to call her so I could actually

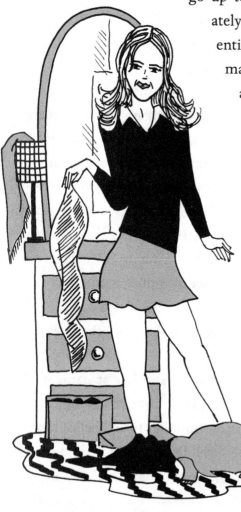

go up to her apartment, I immediately received high fives from the entire door staff. Feeling like the man, I summoned the elevator and proceeded on up to the tenth floor.

When I walked into her apartment, what I saw has been permanently burned into my mind. It was nothing like I had imagined it would be; in my fantasy she opened the door and there was a beautiful table with fresh-cut flowers with a lovely mirror hanging above it so I could check out my hair. No table with fresh flowers greeted me. Instead I saw a half-open closet with dirty clothes and clean dry cleaning spilling out into the entrance. I had hoped for an elegant living room with a flat-screen TV and a perfectly positioned couch that could support the fifty different sexual positions I had planned for us that night (sorry to be crude, but this is what your next Mr. Right Now will be thinking as he fantasizes about your "dinner and a movie invite").

Unfortunately, all I saw were things for sale and lots and lots of boxes. Her apartment looked like the set of "Sanford and Son." Everything she owned seemed to be for sale, which immediately made me think the following: "She's a fugitive on the run who needs money for a plane ticket to Guam, she has credit-card debt and is fighting off personal bankruptcy, or she has a small drug problem and she is trying to round up money for her next fix." And to make matters worse, her television was a little larger than an iPhone and was located on the floor, where she had so considerately put down two oversized pillows and two little dinner placemats.

I remember thinking, "Well, we still have the bedroom, the place that is sacred and special to all women." As we stumbled over the boxes nearing her bedroom, I still had a ray of hope, but when she opened the door, my final hope was crushed. Her bedroom looked like a crack den. All I saw was a mattress—just a mattress; no box springs, bed frame, or headboard. The mattress didn't even have real sheets on it. Instead, it was covered by some kind of throw blanket. Two milk crates served as nightstands. She kept her workout clothes, panties, and T-shirts in plastic shelves from the Container Store. There was no indication that a female lived on the premises; there were no pictures on the walls, pretty smells, or delicate furniture.

It really wasn't until later in the evening that I understood why Tamsen was living the way she was. Her focus was completely on her career, and falling in love was the last thing on her mind. Tamsen was in transition at the time, and the condition of her place was only a temporary state. That night we connected on every level imaginable, and by morning her apartment was a complete afterthought. I didn't run for the door, but I wouldn't have blamed any guy who might have done just that. Luckily, Tamsen waited a relatively long time to invite me to her place. By the time I finally did get a load of where she lived, I was already hooked. But if it had been earlier in the game, chances are I would have bolted. To this day, the shock of what I saw when she first opened the door renders me speechless; so much so that I must turn it over now to Tamsen.

 In my defense, I must say that my apartment was in a supercool building in Old City, Philadelphia. It had hardwood floors, an adorable black-and-white-tiled bathroom, and huge floor-to-ceiling windows overlooking a marketplace called Head House Square. I loved it. The problem was I spent very little time there, and I was in a serious mental transition. My goal was to leave Philadelphia for New York City. I didn't have a job or a job offer yet, but I knew that the move was what I wanted, so I decided to do a lit-

tle "shedding." Plus, I was never too worried about the whole interior decorating thing. I mean, how many sets of sheets do you really need? So, I had put half of my belongings on sale on eBay, and the other half were packed away "just in case."

In addition, I had demanding hours. I worked all day and went away whenever I wanted. And quite frankly, I was in no way trying to impress a guy. The last thing I was thinking about was how much Matt would like my place or how it would reflect on me. But looking back, I realize that my apartment was for functionality and not for living. I dressed to impress, but when it came to my house it told guys I was not interested, couldn't care less if they were in my life, and had no room for them or any type of commitment. I'm thankful Matt was willing to overlook the vibe I was sending out. Today, I can't wait to decorate my place. I give serious thought to everything I put in it and make sure it represents who I am and what I want to tell the world. I never realized how important it was to a man that I had certain things in my place to show him where I was in life.

• BUILDING A GUY-FRIENDLY LOVE SHACK •

If you think your home needs some work to be guy friendly, not to worry; we have simplified things for you by going from room to room to tell you what you should keep, lose, or add to your place.

You don't need to hire an expensive decorator or spend hours walking around home improvement stores trying to look like someone you're not. These are just simple suggestions that can help you add to your place and keep Mr. Right Now from running out the door before he has the chance to really get to know you.

The Living Room Shopping List

At first, you will probably spend a majority of your time in the living room with Mr. Right Now. To make sure you are prepared, here are a few items to add to your living room so that you don't have to go thrashing around in a closet to find something upon his arrival:

✦ **A blanket:** Tuck it under the couch and make sure it's easily accessible. If he comes over one night and you want to cuddle under it, you want to make sure it smells good and can be found without drama.

✦ **Candles:** You can get a few small ones or one big one, and that will do the trick. Make sure you have matches or a lighter close by. You don't want it to look like a cliché seduction scene, but you do want to make sure you have all the elements in place, just in case.

✦ **Guy-friendly DVDs:** When you find these on sale, pick them up and add them to your home movie collection. Examples include *The Godfather, Scarface, Old School,* and *Wedding Crashers.*

✦ **Firewood (if you have a fireplace)**: In the winter months, there is nothing like a romantic fire that you can just "throw together."

The Kitchen Shopping List

The items in your fridge and pantry should be staples for you, but here are the right things to have on hand just in case he stops by:

- ✦ Bottled water
- ✦ Soda (diet and regular)
- ✦ Beer
- ✦ Wine (unopened)
- ✦ Apples or pears
- ✦ Cheese
- ✦ Assorted crackers (not Saltines)
- ✦ Walnuts/dried apricots (for a quick cheese plate)
- ✦ Mixed nuts
- ✦ Peppermint candy (to deal with any breath issues)
- ✦ Coffee (for the morning)
- ✦ Powdered creamer (so you don't have to worry about milk spoiling)
- ✦ Bagels or bread of your choice (frozen, so you can keep it for a long time)

+ Butter (can also freeze and defrost before the date)
+ Something sweet to eat

The Love Nest Shopping List

Your bedroom is the room that thrives on the power of sugges-
tion. A man believes he can tell volumes about a woman the
moment he enters her bedroom. In this place, his mind starts
racing, wondering all sorts of things, from how you look naked
to how he will perform in the sack. The bedroom carries a lot
of weight; a lot of serious stuff is going to happen in there, so
make sure that yours is well equipped before you get too far
into the game. The bedroom is also a place for you to create
your own sense of sensuality and identity. He needs to work to
get to it, and once he's there, he needs to worship you because
you are a princess, and he has just entered your chambers.

Some details that will make your bedroom ready for
anything:

+ Candles
+ Fresh-cut flowers
+ No books in sight (they can be shelved; the self-help ones
  should be hidden)
+ A variety of outfits (boy shorts and a tank, lingerie, and
  two robes, one silk, one cotton)
+ Fresh sheets
+ Sexy throw pillows

The side drawer should contain:

◆ Breath mints
◆ Massage oil
◆ Any other pertinent items that HE would enjoy. (The toy
collection should be hidden unless he asks for it.)

THE LOVE SHACK QUIZ

1. What is the first thing you see upon entering your apartment or home?

    a. Your favorite Bon Jovi poster from junior high school
    b. A beautiful vase filled with fresh-cut flowers
    c. The newest Sony 57″ plasma television
    d. All seven of your beloved cats

2. The one word that best describes your current dwelling is:

    a. Grand
    b. Musty
    c. Cluttered
    d. Sleek

3. Which magazine is displayed on your coffee table?

    a. *National Enquirer*
    b. *Vanity Fair*
    c. *Guns & Ammo*
    d. *Pageantry Magazine*

(continued)

4. Your living room rugs are made from which material?

    a. Soft Oriental silk
    b. Acrylic
    c. Rubber
    d. What living room rugs?

5. What is the one thing that is always easily visible in your bathroom?

    a. SpongeBob bubble bath
    b. Clean, fresh candles
    c. Castor oil bottle
    d. Moldy shower curtain

6. If you had to leave your apartment or home in a hurry and take just one item with you, what would it be?

    a. My black velvet Elvis painting
    b. My sterling silver framed family photo
    c. My *Star Wars* action figure collection
    d. My toothbrush

7. Where did you buy your home's furniture?

    a. IKEA
    b. I found it on the street
    c. Private estate sale
    d. Crate and Barrel/Pottery Barn

8. In my refrigerator you'll always find . . .

    a. Beer
    b. Fine, aged cheese
    c. Six-week-old takeout
    d. Jell-O chocolate pudding cups

9. Your dream home would be something like:

  a. The Taj Mahal
  b. Disney's Haunted Mansion
  c. Buckingham Palace
  d. The Four Seasons Hotel

10. What is the first emotion you feel when entering your home?

  a. Joy
  b. Comfort
  c. Fear
  d. Confusion

You're a class act if you chose: 1. b, 2. d, 3. b, 4. a, 5. b, 6. b, 7. d, 8. b, 9. d, 10. a

The place you call home is a reflection of who you are. And now that you're a smokin' hot Bond Girl, your pad should be Bond Girl worthy! But that's not the only reason to take our advice and build a rockin' Love Shack. It's not just about getting the guy; it's also about figuring out how to mesh your life with Mr. Right. So roll out the welcome mat and create an environment that's sure to keep him coming back for more!

4

WHERE THE BOYS ARE

Hey, you! Yeah, you, the hottie sitting around your apartment in the Juicy Couture sweatpants complaining to your girlfriends about all the loser guys in your town. Put down the glass of merlot, and snuff out that cigarette—you don't even smoke! Enough with the drama! If you don't take some serious action, the ghost from "spinster future" will be tapping you on the shoulder in thirty years when your Friday nights consist of Nell, your roommate, nagging you to put on your housecoat so you can go to the kitchen and feed your ten cats. Seriously, though, Mr. Right ain't poppin' in anytime soon. You need to take that smokin' body of yours out the door with a couple of your hot friends, and even a few of your semihot ones (they'll make you look even hotter—sorry, I'm a guy, just bein' honest!), and get to the right places to find your man. Your future love connection is on the move; he is living his life, and you need to catch him in the act.

My female matchmaking clients are constantly asking me where to find eligible men and what to do when they see one. In this chapter, Tamsen and I will arm you with all you need to know about *where* to meet the guys as well as *what* to do when you spot one who piques your interest. The chapter contains a list of places where guys hang, congregate, and socialize. In addition, we'll help you work with all the tools available to you, such as Internet dating sites and professional services like ours, as you start out on your search.

But we don't intend to leave you in the lurch. What good is catching the man of your dreams if you don't know how to reel him in! To that end, we'll also give you guidance on what to do once you've found your guy.

However, before we delve into the list, here's a little something I'd like you to remember: the more "meat market–like" the environment, the lower the quality of the people you'll meet there and the higher the risk of becoming involved in a one-night stand. The truth is that more natural, uncontrived environments set the stage for meaningful, lasting relationships. Examples of highly contrived environments are bars, speed-dating events, and Internet dating sites. Some find that dating services can

also seem contrived, however, quality dating services can lead you to Mr. Right. Trust me; I have seen it with my own eyes. In this chapter, we'll show you how. And considering Internet dating is here to stay, we're also going to show you how to make it work for you. The trick to any successful guy search is, no matter how you decide to approach it, be patient. The right guy is out there, you just have to find him.

THE SINGLE GIRL'S DAILY TREASURE HUNT

Ladies, men are not hard to find. In fact, you are surrounded by them, so stop wasting time complaining about being single, and start tuning into your surroundings. You'll be surprised at what you see. It doesn't matter if you live in New York City or Spokane, Washington—men are everywhere. The first step is opening your mind and heart to meeting the man of your dreams. But I'll be straight with you: finding a guy can be a full-time job, and finding a great guy can be near impossible unless you are open to every opportunity that crosses your path. The little old lady you help cross the street could have a gorgeous, 6'2" grandson she is just dying to introduce to someone. Or the man who asks for directions could eventually find his way to asking you out. We have already told you how to dress for a man and how to fix up your place for one. Now we are going to tell you how to find one. Below are some of the most popular places to meet a great man. We've even divided these locales into age-appropriate places to help you narrow down your search for Mr. Right.

Got Chores?

According to a recent study, more than 50 percent of all couples met each other while running an errand. These people were not dressed to impress, nor did they plan on finding "the one" that day. It just happened. This is why contrived environments such as bars, lounges, or singles events can ultimately be big disappointments. When you walk into a bar, it's obvious everyone is clinging to a bar stool straining to get a gander at the next person who walks in. Many women get all dolled up and spend their Friday and Saturday nights hopping from one bar to another, hoping to find Mr. Right. Most go home disappointed. So, don't wait for your weekend bar-hopping extravaganza to start your guy search. Start today with your trip to the dry cleaners.

I'm not saying you have to be dressed to the nines to run your errands; just look respectable and be aware of who is around you. Some of the places that seem like a hassle could actually turn out to be quite enjoyable if you are in the right frame of mind. The post office, laundry mat, drugstore, video store, and grocery store—any of these places could be where you meet your future love.

Line Up

Speaking of grocery stores, surprisingly, a majority of men say standing in line is a great place to meet a woman. When you think about it, it makes perfect sense. Men feel comfortable when they instantly have something in common with you. The fact that both of you are standing in an annoying line is common ground and can act as an icebreaker. You know the saying "Misery loves company." Well, in this instance it should be changed to "Misery makes company." Men standing in line are more willing to start a conversation with a stranger in order to pass the time (and perhaps get you to pass over your number). So, don't just stand there and fantasize about the great butt in front of you; do something about it! When he smiles at you—and you know he will—make a comment about what he is purchasing, and start the conversation.

Need a Ride?

Crowded subway cars, buses, or trains can all be vehicles for love. Case in point: one of our clients was distraught over a man she had been seeing. Every Friday she'd make the trip to New York City to see this guy who barely gave her the time of day. They would spend a rather lonely weekend together having horrible sex and empty conversation, and then she would hop on the train back to Philadelphia feeling very unsure of herself, the relationship, and whether she would ever find true love.

One Sunday, as she sat on the train, she realized she was surrounded by a number of great-looking men. She turned off her iPod and started talking to a guy across the aisle. She was having such a good time that she nearly missed her stop and almost ended up in Washington, D.C. The experience made her realize all of the opportunities that she had been missing. During her commute, she was always thinking about the guy in NYC instead of checking out the potential all around her on the train. The realization that the world is full of cute, single guys led her to break it off with Mr. Wrong. Believe it or not, she met her husband on the commute back from the breakup weekend! A little train tip: Amtrak is a favorite for meeting guys; the trains are usually full of professionals on their way home from business trips, and there's a car where you can grab a drink. Plus, the close quarters are a great excuse for men and women to talk and flirt without the anxiety of approaching one another without a reason.

Find a Sport and Suit Up

If you aren't the athletic type, this may not be for you. But if you like to sweat it out after work and on the weekends, why not take on a co-ed, team sport. Singles and co-ed team sports make for a winning combination. It's a good way to truly get to know someone and let your guard down. It's hard to be fake when you're whacking a ball and trying to steal second base. Co-ed sports allow you to get to know people much faster, and you get to see them interact with others. An added benefit: when men and women are playing together in a competitive way, the sexual tension builds naturally, and before you know it they are players in their own game of love. Some examples of popular co-ed sports are kickball, dodgeball, softball, flag football, and volleyball. Find a league through work, your local community center, your church, or your gym and sign up. And don't show up in old sweats and dirty sneakers. Rock some cute, athletic outfits that show off your sporty side.

Puppy Love

Let's face it. Sometimes a girl's best friend weighs about five pounds and can fit inside of her Pucci dog-carrying bag. Loving, loyal, and ever the best listeners, our pups have seen our fair-weather friends come and go and have secretly done the happy dance when we kicked our last boyfriend to the curb. Large or small, furry or not, these constant companions are the one warm body we can always find in our beds at night. And the best part is that your pup can double as a guy magnet: guys dig dogs. Guys dig chicks with dogs. Now it's time for your precious pooch to carry his weight. Throw on your sneakers, grab the leash and some treats, and head out for a long walk. You will have men stopping at every turn to pat your pooch on the head, and perhaps one or two of them will stop to pant over you. Another great way to use your dog to meet a guy is to take him or her to the dog park. Dog parks are great places to meet single guys. As I mentioned, it's much easier on guys when there's common ground to strike up a conversation. Your mutual love for canines is just the thing to break the ice.

Coffee and Sushi Bars

These are great spots for meeting guys because it's perfectly acceptable to sit at a coffee bar or a sushi bar alone. And single men love these venues because they're teaming with life. It's hard to feel lonely when you're surrounded by dozens of people. And the old "common ground" theory applies here too; it's easy to strike up a conversation with someone about coffee or sushi.

Charity Events/Volunteer Groups

If you like to volunteer or attend charity functions, it stands to reason that you would want to be with someone who enjoys them as well. I've found that single women have amazing success meeting men when they volunteer with groups that build houses, fix up parks, or work in soup kitchens. Being charitable not only gives back to the community, it may also give you a date for next Friday night!

Gadget Stores

If you're ever bored on a Saturday afternoon, wander over to your local gadget store and you will quickly see where all the men are hiding. Guys love gadgets because they allow them to act like eight-year-olds again. Mega computer stores, cell phone stores, stereo shops, and places like Brookstone and Sharper Image have actually put out displays so that you can quickly locate the single guy of your choice. Just kidding. But seriously, the gadgets have a relaxing effect on men, so they're more liable to have their guards down and strike up a conversation with you.

Running Clubs

I know we mentioned taking up a sport, but running clubs can be even more intimate than team sports. Members of running clubs meet weekly, but many of the avid runners pair off during the week to get in more miles. To get the most mileage out of a club like this one, make sure fellow members know you are serious about taking up running, and don't complain when you're there. If you decide to join, don't go there to play "the dumb girl" or you won't be able to find out "where the boys ran" to get away from you. And if you join, make sure you can keep up; there's nothing more unattractive than a sweaty, out-of-breath woman collapsed in a heap on the side of a running path.

・・・・・ WHERE THE BOYS ARE BY AGE ・・・・・

I just mentioned some of the places where you can meet men; now I want to break it down even further by age. Twenty-five-year-olds have different interests than forty-five-year-olds. Here are the top-ten places in each age demographic where single women meet fabulous men.

Ages Twenty-Five to Thirty

1. Through your friends and family (Make sure every single one of them knows you are single; it takes a village to meet a guy.)
2. Gym (This means no stained T-shirts and ripped sweats; look your sporty best.)
3. Running club
4. Beach
5. Ski resort
6. Parties (Get out there, girl!)
7. Walking your dog (Borrow a friend's pooch if you don't have one.)
8. Graduate school (Especially male-dominated programs, such as MBA programs.)
9. Sporting events (Or sports bars when the big game is on; this is an especially hot spot in bigger cities like NYC.)
10. Speed dating
11. Bookstores and music stores
12. The Apple Store/Sharper Image/Brookstone (Electronics and gadgets turn men into boys.)

Ages Thirty to Forty

1. Eating out with friends (Look around at the other tables, and make sure you don't act like it's a private

party. This is easier to do at restaurants that are livelier or eateries that have communal seating, a growing trend these days.)

2. Singles adventure trips/vacations
3. Classes (cooking/wine tasting/computer)
4. Co-ed softball/volleyball league
5. Whole Foods/Trader Joe's (high-end supermarkets with prepared and gourmet food)
6. Church groups/synagogues
7. Through coworkers and friends
8. Saturday or Sunday mornings at Home Depot (Just wander the aisles!)
9. Matchmaking services (They're superefficient, and you don't have to do the dirty work searching for the right person.)
10. Running club (training for a 5K/10K/marathon)
11. Volunteer groups
12. Bowling alley/roller-skating rinks/ice-skating rinks/the zoo

Over Forty

1. Home Depot or Lowe's on weekends
2. Tech conferences (Get wired, ladies!)
3. Airplanes/trains (Go business or first class when possible—Amtrak's Acela Express is fantastic for meeting this age group!)
4. Matchmaking services

5. Singles dinner clubs/wine tastings

6. Toy stores and parks (Single dads often take kids here on the weekends.)

7. High-end charity events

8. Church groups/synagogues

9. Single parent groups

10. Whole Foods, Trader Joe's

11. Hire a personal trainer (Chances are he is training single men he could introduce you to; if not, at least you are taking care of yourself and staying in shape.)

12. Book parties, art museum openings, city events (See and be seen, everywhere!)

MATCHMAKING OR DATING SERVICES

For some people matchmaking and dating services are just as necessary as their personal trainer, dry cleaner, and housekeeper. As they're making their way up the corporate ladder, many young professionals simply don't have time to go on a search for Mr. or Miss Right.

If you choose to hire a matchmaker as opposed to a dating service, you must be patient. It may take longer to find your match, but your chances of clicking with that person are greater. Also, make sure you choose a matchmaker with experience and a solid reputation. Here are some benefits and drawbacks of each.

MATCHMAKING

Benefits	Drawbacks
Matchmakers personally meet, interact, and get to know the people they are setting up.	It can take time to find a perfect match because it is a smaller pool of people.
You get the information from the matchmaker, not your potential date; that's a good thing considering people often give misleading or downright incorrect information about themselves.	It can be more expensive than a dating service.

DATING SERVICES

Benefits	Drawbacks
Members choose their dates themselves.	You have to rely on the information provided by the person.
It is less expensive than a matchmaker.	You can easily be overlooked if your dating requirements are too specific because it narrows down the dating pool you have to choose from.

ONLINE DATING: GEORGE CLOONEY OR GEORGE COSTANZA?

Posted profile:

Name: Joe

Age: 35

Description: Tall, dark, handsome

Occupation: Doctor

Salary: 500K

Hobbies: Cooking, traveling, working out, spending time at home, being in love

What I Want: A wonderful woman who will be a great mother to our children

Doesn't this profile sound perfect? He's just the kind of guy your mother always told you you would meet! Plus, he sent you a "wink" and he's online! Suddenly, a message pops up on your screen. Here's how the conversation goes.

He types: "Hello, beautiful!"

You type: "Hello."

He types: "Love your picture. Tell me a little something about yourself."

You type: "Like what? The most important thing that I look for in a guy is him being NORMAL! Plus, I need him to be independently wealthy, have model-like looks, and of course treat me like a princess. (LOL)"

He types: "Check, check, and check!! My trust fund was just turned over to me, I used to model for Calvin Klein, and my middle name is Chivalrous. . . . When can we meet?"

You type: "Very nice! You pass! I am free Wednesday night for a drink."

He types: "Perfect!"

Three days later, your hands are sweating as you wait outside the bar where you agreed to meet. In your mind you are thinking, "This could be the last first date that I might have to go on. He could be 'the one'!" You frantically search the eyes of each and every person who comes in and out of the restaurant, eager to cast your eyes on the George Clooney look-alike you fished out from the millions of profiles on the Internet.

Then, someone calls your name; slowly you turn your head. Instead of George Clooney, it's George Costanza who's showed up to meet you for a drink. By the end of a long grueling night, you realize the picture he posted was from fifteen years ago and this is the profile he *meant* to type:

Name: Burt

Age: 46

Description: Short, balding, and bitter

Occupation: In between jobs

Salary: Not currently receiving one

Hobbies: Spending time at home . . . eating!

What I Want: Anyone with a pulse

Sound familiar? Dating online does not necessarily keep people "in line" when it comes to posting accurate, up-to-date information about themselves. Here is my take on the world of high-tech dating: it can be the most efficient and successful way to attempt to find love or one of the most frustrating. Online dating is truly a numbers game. The faster you are able to find out what kind of person your potential love interest really is at the other end of the keyboard, the more efficient you'll become at it.

As this example points out, the biggest problem with online dating is that people misrepresent themselves to become more marketable to potential love interests. Like you, I don't get why online daters lie about the way they look, their jobs, or anything else. You're going to meet them eventually, and the jig will be up. I suppose many of them do it to stroke their egos and live out their fantasy lives in cyberspace. Whatever the reason, the lies and misrepresentations waste your time and often are responsible for landing you in awkward situations. Here are a few pointers for not wasting your time looking for love on the Web, because despite the deceptions and pitfalls, it *is* possible to meet a significant other online, especially since the practice has become perfectly acceptable in this day and age.

The Rules of the Keyboard

1. **Stop wasting time.** This means that if you are chatting with someone, you should not wait until you are all out of keystrokes to meet the person. I say no more than a week of cyber chatting with someone you haven't met. This is not to say run out and meet the guy that night, but make sure you don't encourage a relationship via the Internet, because some guys eventually become too lazy to meet you if you let it drag out long enough.

2. **Do not, under any circumstances whatsoever, go out with a guy the first night you start chatting with him.** A majority of men are online for a one-night stand. Despite what their profiles might say, they are only looking for Miss Right Now. This means they will not be there to cyber chat with you the next day if you make yourself available at the first sign of an invite. I don't care if he tells you he is leaving the country and it's the last time he can see you, or that he has sick relatives living on another planet he needs to go visit. *Do not meet a man you meet online the first night. Period.*

3. **Ask for a photo with a date on it.** Remember, we all looked great when we were twenty years old, but things change, gravity takes hold, and before you know it you're sitting at din-

ner with a man who looks like your father's father. This may sound superficial or downright rude, but it's imperative that you know who you are spending your time with, even if it's simply time spent pecking away at the keyboard.

4. **Once you have made the date, call him at work and at home, just to make sure things add up.** You want to be sure that he's on the up and up and not feeding you a load of fiction. Unfortunately, when it comes to online dating, you often have to play detective just to make sure all the data he's dishing out adds up.

5. **Finally, when you meet, if there is no chemistry, be honest and move on.**

Ladies, get off that couch, grab your pup or one of your cute, single girlfriends, and get yourself out there! You have no more excuses. You now know that available men are everywhere. So open your eyes and your mind to the possibility of finding Mr. Right. The best part of the deal is that the search is rewarding in and of itself. Instead of sitting on your duff lamenting your singleness, you'll find yourself out in the world living your life and adding to your list of fun, fulfilling life experiences.

5

GETTING HIM TO ASK YOU OUT

Who has it worse: the guy sitting in the bar waiting to summon enough courage to approach a woman in the hopes that he has interpreted her flirty looks as an invitation to introduce himself or the woman waiting for that guy to approach her after she has exercised every "subtle" gesture short of throwing her drink at him to get him to introduce himself?

It's a toss-up. Bottom line: waiting sucks! Nonetheless, I do sympathize with women on this one because it does seem easier to go after what you want as opposed to sitting around hoping that what you want finds you. And although it's true that men like to be the aggressors, sometimes they just can't figure out how to make the first move. Unfortunately, when it comes to women, men can be pretty weak—their egos are as fragile as a piece of blown glass. Don't be fooled by the sarcastic guys with the loud personalities and playerlike tendencies. Often, these men are overcompensating for their lack of confidence when it comes to the opposite sex and, quite frankly, life in general.

So there you are, waiting and wondering what's going on in his mind. Exactly what is that cute guy at the bar or in line at the grocery store thinking? Being the turncoat that I am, I'm going to let you into that mind of his. By truly knowing what's going on in his head you'll be two steps ahead of him when he does finally walk over to you.

HIS THOUGHTS

"I've been here for two hours with my friends and made three full trips around the bar checking out 'the talent' [translation:

ladies], but I still think that chick near the front door is the hottest thing in here. One more beer, then I go in for the kill; don't want to feel any pain when I'm talking to her! Man is she hot. Problem is, she talked to at least six guys and none of them has been able to close the deal with her. Hmmm, what's up with her? I counted her checking me out three times. My buddy saw her checking me out too. I don't know, though. OK, let me finish this brew, almost ready to make my move. Wait, what am I thinking? What time is it? I've got to make sure it's close to when I'm ready to bolt 'cause if I commit to trying to take this girl home, and a hotter one walks in, that will suck. There it was—she just looked at me again! Damn, I have to go now before she takes off. I'll smile first to see how she reacts. OK, here I go (brain to mouth: 'SMILE!'). Uh, maybe that wasn't so good; she just stared at me and bit her lower lip. No smile. Wow, maybe I read her wrong? Should I rethink this? Whoa, look at that chick that just walked in. I think she just checked me out! Maybe I should go talk to her. . . . "

So, while you're patiently standing around trying to keep up your come-hither look, the wheels in his brain are barely turning. Allow me to add a few more insights to this scenario:

✦ **When men go out in groups, they rarely leave the safety of their herd to hook up with one girl.** There is an unspoken understanding that they are out to be with the boys, and any attention they give women is purely to show off or to entertain the other Neanderthals in the group.

✦ **Men are no good at detecting subtle cues from women.** This is something that constantly surprises me. My theory is that men are so blindingly insecure that they literally can't see the cues. Remember how hard it was for the guy in the scenario to believe that the woman in the bar was interested in him, even though she couldn't have made it any more obvious—from the forty-five solid minutes of blatant staring to the inviting smiles to the classic "I want you so bad I could taste you" lip bite. The guy was simply too insecure to believe that such a beautiful girl could be interested in him.

✦ **Men suffer from something that I call "the next best thing syndrome."** They believe that no matter how incredibly beautiful, interesting, and sexy the woman in front of them is, a more beautiful, more interesting, and sexier woman is waiting around the corner. I believe the next best thing syndrome is actually a defense mechanism. Men do this to avoid putting any "emotional skin" in the game with one woman. Think about it. A man's genetic predisposition commands that he put his "mark" on as many women as possible. It's a drive that even plays out during a simple night out with the boys. In a situation like the one described, that mark is usually some banal, ridiculously unintelligent conversation that ends with a woman feeling incredibly let down. And the guy usually ends up going home alone and gratifying himself in a lonely studio apartment in a bad section of town.

✦ **Men have a special formula that they use to decide if they will approach a woman who has piqued their interest.** Here's how the formula works: the more attractive the woman, the more hoops the man has to jump through to sleep with her. Guys in general can be extremely lazy. So when a guy sees a girl he is interested in, he turns into a human computer and calculates the risk versus reward ratio associated with the time and energy that will be necessary to get the girl into bed. When a gorgeous woman is staring, smiling, or otherwise throwing herself at a guy and he is just standing there playing pocket pool, it might very well be that he doesn't want to put forth what he believes will be a tremendous effort to seal the deal. He's much more likely to approach a woman that he's less attracted to because he believes it will take a lot less effort to sleep with her.

THE WAIT IS OVER

The good news is you don't have to sit around and wait for a man to make the first move; you can approach him yourself. But before we show you how to approach a man, it's important to understand that there is a very fine line between getting him to ask you out and asking him out yourself. We don't want you to do the latter. The man should still be the aggressor, but if you wait for some guys to realize that, you will be old and gray before you get a drink date out of them! That's not to say that we want you to go throwing yourself at any guy you see, but there are ways to show him you are open and receptive to him and that you are not going to snuff him out like a cigarette the minute he makes a move in your direction. Remember, you are a confident woman who will never act desperate no matter how hot you are for that guy in the produce aisle. So, we're going to instruct you on how to get a man's attention, perhaps even approach him, but, remember, you will not be asking him out.

 Using case-by-case scenarios I am now going to show you how to get a guy to ask you out. If you find yourself in a situation where you're trying to grab a man's attention or want him to look at you as more than a friend, you need to take some very specific steps; these steps will differ depending on whether he is a stranger versus a friend versus a coworker.

When He Is a Stranger

OK, this guy is a blank slate. You've never seen him before, but he's hot. So, pull yourself together and get ready to go in. You have nothing to lose. If he is receptive, you will completely stand out and be someone that he most likely will never forget no matter where the relationship goes. If he is cold and unresponsive, who cares, it has *nothing* to do with you. Do not take it personally. Any guy who doesn't appreciate a strange woman approaching him to get to know him better is not a man. He is more like an insecure boy.

You want to be concerned with making sure you take the right approach. Remember, not too many women approach guys they don't know. The first thing you need to do is to take in your immediate environment, the one thing that at the moment you have in common with him. If you're standing in a grocery line, comment about the checkout girl, his groceries, or how overpriced the store is. Always try to put a positive spin on anything you comment on. Better yet, ask him a question. Men are still suckers for the "Damsel in Distress" card. This is a nice technique to use because it balances out the fact that you took the "aggressive role" in approaching him by immediately showing him a passive feminine need for him. In response, he will somehow become a complete authority on whatever question you have asked him.

During his lengthy dissertation on, let's say, soy milk (remember you're in a grocery line), your nonverbal cues must be right on. So, make sure to do the following:

✦ **Do not lose eye contact with him at any time during the conversation.** Allow your eyes to stay on his a split second longer than normal.

✦ **Subtly work your hair.** If it's long, twist it, swing it, put it behind your ear in that sexy way. If it's short, gaze downward and simultaneously run your hand through it and look right into his eyes when you raise your head.

✦ **Let him talk.** You asked the question, so be an attentive listener. Don't hang on his every word, but do comment on his answers.

✦ **When you respond to his answer or comment on something, make sure you touch his shoulder or forearm.** This will give him the underlying message that you really could not care less about the soy milk.

✦ **After he answers your question, it's OK to change the subject and inconspicuously look for other commonalities you might share with him.** For example, ask him if this is the only place he shops, and tell him you shop here because it's close to your house. He will most likely answer you and also volunteer where he lives. You can then in turn say that you run along the river path right near his house, which gives him the opportunity to tell you that he runs on the same path. Then, you can say you need a running partner because you go late and maybe he could apply for that position. He will accept because you have been cute, confident, and most important, unique (because you approached him). So, now you have a date, all because of soy milk.

When He Simply Won't

Meet Mr. Mental Brick Wall. You've used all your best signals (and listened to all our advice), and he still won't take that leap and say "Hello." As a matter of fact he can barely do anything around you. Is this a sign that he's head over heels or just a heel?

It's pretty clear that guys have insecurities about approaching women, but what isn't so clear is how they play out for each man. If the guy, who is about as talkative as the Frankenstein monster, still shows no interest in you, then you are going to have to make like a crowd of angry villagers and storm his castle. You will need to make the first move and see if he responds. If he overcomes his shyness and turns out to be an intelligent and charming conversationalist, then good job. But if you find only another monster lurking in the shadows—namely the man who wants the perfect fantasy woman and won't settle for anyone, anytime, anywhere—run the other way. Why this guy even goes out is a mystery to me. He should just stay in and wait for his *Sports Illustrated* swimsuit model to find him, ring his doorbell, and pledge eternal love to him. I mean, it's his destiny, right? Give me a break!

Also keep in mind that there is a chance that the drop-dead gorgeous man at the coffee shop whom you keep smiling at is waiting for his . . . boyfriend, so chalk it up to genetics and hope he has a straight brother somewhere.

Finally, a guy might not approach you because you simply don't interest him. And guess what? That's cool too. Chemistry is a must. Without it, there's no shot for a match. Not gonna happen. If that hunk sitting alone likes blondes and you're a redhead, let it go. What are you going to do, run out and buy a wig? Guys like what they like, just as you like what you like. So, stay focused on finding the guy who will return your interest and desire with his own.

When He Is Online

 If the guy is someone you know from the "real world," such as a friend of a friend you met once at a party, and you have always wanted to approach him in person and you have his e-mail address, then a little cyber hello is a great thing. In this case, though, make sure it's a very generic hello that says something to the effect of, "Do you run in Washington Park? I think I have seen you there." If he is receptive and asks you a few questions, then feel free to continue chatting to see if he asks you out. But if he replies with a rather cool "Yes," then delete his e-mail from your address book.

This brings us to our next category: a handsome man whose profile you have stumbled across on an Internet dating site. Surely, he can't be this perfect. Put your guard up with Mr. TooGood2BTrue. That sexy hunk with all the right answers might just be a total fraud. Online connections are full of possible traps if you don't know who is on the other side of the keyboard. So, we want you to proceed with caution when it comes to getting a guy to ask you out in this arena. As we told you in Chapter 4, there are lots of pros and success stories with online dating, but there are also some serious cons (literally). In fact, the outcome can be anything from wedding bells to a date from hell. Check out my little list of pros and cons:

The Pros: Right Clicking Your Way to Romance

+ You don't have to waste precious nights at your local happy hour. Instead, with one swipe of a keystroke you can download your list of Mr. Desirables and wait for the replies to start piling into your inbox.

+ It's easy to flirt from behind a computer screen, and you don't have to get all dressed up to do it!

+ You can be 100 percent selective in your search, right down to the type of shoes he prefers.

+ It can be fun and stress-free, because you are meeting multiple prospects instead of putting all of your date dresses in one basket.

+ You can retain your privacy because you decide how much or how little to tell someone.

But with the good comes the bad. Read on.

The Cons: Sex, Lies, and Your Computer Screen

+ Online dating can be a serious time waster because men and women often look for different things online. Many men tend to look for sex, while women are looking for love.

+ It can be a full-time job. There are lots of messages to reply to, and you have to take time to delete the frogs before you can save a prince.

+ It can be dangerous if you hand out too much personal information, so you are often monitoring what you are dispensing.

+ People can easily misrepresent themselves online with old pictures, old information, or worse, a fake profile with someone else's information on it!

✦ It can keep you single for a long time because you spend countless hours in front of the computer screen instead of getting back out there and meeting people and experiencing life live and in person.

Now, let's get back to Mr. TooGood2BTrue and pretend he is indeed true but hasn't yet asked you out. You can send him a message, but make it friendly, not flirty. This means instead of typing, "I love your eyes," ask him more factual questions: "What is your dog's name?" "How long have you lived in Indiana?" "What does your name mean?" Doing this will not only set you apart from the rest of the girls e-mailing him but will also give him a chance to talk with you instead of flirt with you. The relationship will start with substance instead of coy little comments. If he doesn't answer you, don't keep e-mailing him. Move on to the next profile. There are plenty of fish in the sea, but the pool of men dating online is even bigger!

When He Is a Coworker

That sexy new guy three cubicles over is ruining your usual workday routine. Instead of getting those reports done, you're constantly sneaking glances at him. It'd be so much easier if he just came over and asked you out for a coffee or lunch.

Haven't you been reading? Hello! The guy obviously needs a little push before he suavely swings over for an introduction. Like all successful working women you are going to need to do your homework. Try to find out some information about where he came from, who he's working with, and, of course, if he's in a relationship. Once you've got some info to go on, put yourself in his line of vision; keep that body front and center. Take a stroll past his workstation, and don't put your head down when you do. Let him know you'd like to promote him to a "new position." Maybe even more than one! Seriously, make yourself a part of his visual day at work. And because some guys might have anxiety about making bold moves at the office, a bit of cunning on your part may be in order. Try this sneaky little move: leave a folder meant for you on his desk. Giving him a legitimate reason to approach you will provide the perfect opening. It allows him to break the ice without having to make a full-on first move. When he does return that "project folder" you desperately needed, don't let him get away without a proper thank-you. Offer to buy him a cup of coffee or, if he's a transplant, offer to take him around town to check out a few of your favorite haunts. But make sure you plan a day trip as opposed to an evening out on the town—that would be perceived as being too forward. Remember, there's a fine line between getting him to ask you out and throwing your naked self into his arms.

When He Is Just a Friend

 You know the story: friends first, lovers later. Many of the most successful couples we know started out as best buds before taking it to the next step. Allow me to set the scene. It's the usual weekend meet-up at your place before your gang hits the bars, clubs, or wherever, but tonight you want to end up in the arms of your guy pal, let's call him "Michael," instead of at the diner with your wing girls. You've been noticing how cute Michael is, you've been thinking about him a lot lately, and he's single too. You share tons of the same interests and have real affection for each other. That's a good start, but here's where you need to turn up the heat to make sure he is into you too.

Make sure you are dressed to impress. Sex it up a little bit more than usual. If Michael usually sees you in a baseball hat at co-ed softball or in your grungy old sweats when everyone gets together to watch the game, change it up a bit. He needs to stop seeing you like just one of the guys and start seeing you like one of the girls he might want to go out with. Focus on him when he enters the room. Give him a few cues that will put you in a different place in his mind. Brush his arm when he says something funny. Voluntarily get him a drink. Don't even ask him. And lean into him as he updates you on his week. Keep those sexy eyes of yours glued to his. He'll notice the attention.

Once the gang steps out for the night, you'll have to step it up a bit. Your strategy must change direction to keep Michael on his toes. Instead of showering him with special attention, keep a bit of distance when in a public place. Let him wonder where you are. When you do reappear, give him a smile and a nod to let him know that you are there and available, but not too available. You must turn into a woman before his very eyes. This is not about game playing; this is about changing roles in his life so that he can see you as a romantic partner as opposed to a drinking partner. It may take time, but if he picks up on your cues, it could be the beginning of a wonderful relationship that already has a strong foundation: friendship.

One word of caution: DO NOT, under any circumstances, sleep with him sooner than you would sleep with a stranger just because you have been his best bud for three years. This can become a disaster faster than any one-night stand you have ever heard of. If he is a friend and part of a larger group of your friends, a night of sex could make things too awkward for both of you to continue to be around each other in a platonic way. All sorts of ugly things will happen if it doesn't work out and either of you feels used, embarrassed, or like it was simply a huge mistake. The last thing you want is to have sex with a friend one weekend and the next be forced to meet his new girlfriend because he still considers you just a good buddy.

•••••••• A RED FLAG ON THE FIELD ••••••••

It's great when a guy finally overcomes all obstacles and asks you out. But no one wants to waste time. While dating is very much about trial and error, why not avoid situations where a potential match is doomed from the start? You do not want to get a guy to ask you out only to realize right off the bat that he couldn't be more wrong for you. To avoid this, keep an eye out for obvious red flags, which are easy to overlook when you're concentrating on him making the first move.

+ If the guy smokes and you are allergic to smoke or simply hate it, don't look for him to come over and ask for your digits. This is a waste of time; you don't need to spend the next six weeks buying nicotine patches hoping that he will quit.

+ If he's talking to every single woman in the bar, buying them drinks, and being very "hands-on," this is probably not someone who is looking for love. A player like this will leave you constantly wondering what he is up to and who he is going up to. This is a time waster, so move on.

✦ If the guy has children and you are not the maternal type, please leave the fella alone. You are not going to win any points by going gaga over his children at first and then ignoring them the minute he is yours. This is not so much a red flag as it is a warning to be sure of what you want when you are going after it.

✦ If the guy has no job, is living on a friend's couch, and has to borrow his buddy's car to get around, you might not want to get involved. Don't try to save a man. While it's wonderful that you're a kind soul and want to give people a fair chance whether they are at the top of their game or hitting rock bottom, be careful who you attract into your life. Avoid people who will be a drain on you mentally, financially, or otherwise. You want a life partner, not a project for life.

Take all of these "ice-breaking" strategies and put them in your file so that the next time you find yourself in a situation with a Mr. Potential you can take matters into your own capable hands and get the ball rolling. As you now know, there's no need to wait for him to make the first move, but remember to walk that fine line; you can break the ice, but ultimately he has to take the plunge and ask you out.

THE DATE

Once you both like what you see, you most likely will find yourselves on a date. These getting-to-know-you activities may seem harmless—you'll have conversations, eat dinner, take in a show—but beware: communication with guys and dating etiquette are fraught with challenges and potential pitfalls. How should the niceties of the dating cycle proceed? How much should you reveal and when? What intimate matters should you discuss right away? Which ones should you keep in the vault forever? When should you let him in on your deepest and darkest? We've got the answers to all these questions. And to make sure that make-or-break first date is your best show ever, Matt and I have put together a list of first-date guidelines that, if followed, will keep him coming back for seconds, thirds, and fourths.

ACT ONE: FIRST DATE DOS AND DON'TS

1. Don't Touch That Dial

He has asked you out. You are going to get together for drinks and then a quick bite to eat. You set the date on Wednesday for the upcoming Friday night at 8:00 P.M., and you are going to meet at your favorite restaurant in town. But you haven't heard from him since you made the actual plans. What should you do? Send a text, write a quick e-mail, call, or just assume he is going to remember? If you chose the last option, you are correct. You are not going to make any kind of contact with him to remind him that he has a date with you. You set a time. He doesn't need you to be like his mother reminding him not to forget to pick up his socks—or his date—before he goes to bed. Be confident and know that you are fabulous, and there is no way he'll forget tonight's the night.

Besides, most guys have an inflated ego, so he'll interpret one of two things from your contacting him. He may assume that you are totally into him and will be easy to get into the sack. If this is the case, he'll put less effort into trying to impress you because he'll believe you're a sure thing. Or he'll think you're desperate and that you don't have many dates, so this is a very special night for you. He'll then take the position that he is doing you a favor and that you'll be happy with anything he does. Both assumptions will set the stage for his thinking that he dictates the pace and intensity of any potential relationship.

2. Do Dress Comfortably

Don't try your date outfit on for the first time ten minutes before he is scheduled to show up in your lobby. Make sure you've test-driven it at least once. You don't want to take the chance of breaking open your zipper as you hop up onto the barstool to wait for your table. Also, the last thing you want to do is be overdressed or underdressed. If you know he is taking you to an outdoor café and there is a chance the two of you will take a walk afterward, your four-inch stilettos are not going to cut it. If you have plans to go bowling, lose the short skirt. Also remember that the reason he asked you out in the first place is that he thinks you're totally hot, not because he thinks you're a nice person, seem intelligent, and have great moral fiber. He is going on a date with you so he can lust after you all night long. So, please look your best. Flip back to Chapter 2 for more details on how to dress for your date.

3. Do Be on Time

Give yourself enough time to get ready so that you are relaxed and not late! You do not want to keep a guy waiting in your lobby or at a restaurant. He will either think the date wasn't a priority for you or that you are so high maintenance that if he does end up with you, he'll be condemned to a life of waiting. If you are going to meet him at the location, there is no such thing as being "fashionably late." While this might seem cute when you're going to a party or a big event, there's nothing cute about it when you keep a guy waiting outside a bar or restaurant for fifteen minutes. How would you feel if while he was waiting for you, he struck up a conversation with a gorgeous cocktail waitress who was moonlighting while in law school at Harvard, fell madly in love with her, and married her? All because you were five minutes late. Believe me, he is not interested in seeing you sashay into the place, fashionably late, while his drink is making a puddle on the table. Make sure if you agree on a time, you stick to it. In fact, be five minutes early. This is not just a dating rule, it's a life rule.

4. Do Leave It at the Door

The moment has arrived. The sassy little sundress you bought yesterday looks fabulous. Your pedicure dried perfectly. Even your hair looks good despite the fact that there's 90 percent humidity in the air, which usually has you looking like a frizzed-out poodle. You've got it going on. And he's on time. When you hear the bell, you wonder, "Do I ask him in to be polite?" The answer: *Hell no! Leave it at the door.* This is not the time for the grand tour of where you live. On the first date, you must begin and end the date at the door. I don't care if you just purchased the slickest flat-screen TV money can buy, or if you are dying to introduce him to Sparkles, your darling Chihuahua. If he is coming to pick you up, make sure that your purse, keys, and cell phone are by the door so that the second he knocks, you can scoop them up and head out.

If he drops you off after the date, do not invite him inside for an after-dinner drink. If the date went well, there will be a second one, and then you can decide if you want to ask him inside. He doesn't need to see your childhood pictures, your Crate and Barrel purchases, or the fact that you live in a great place. Leaving it at the door is a must. As we made clear in Chapter 3, the minute he enters your home, he will start analyzing you and what you are about. Unravel the mystery of you slowly.

5. Don't Sleep with Him

For a woman, the formative stage of the relationship is the stage in which the guy lusts after her. During the "lusting stage" the woman can take complete control of the budding relationship by *not* giving him sex. I know, I know, a lot of you are saying, "What if that's what I want, too?" My answer: you can give it up quickly and have one great night of passion, then hope that memory will last you 'til the next guy comes along, because the one you just slept with on the first date won't stick around for date #2, or you can *wait* and eventually have tons of great sex with this guy who might actually turn out to be "the one."

Here is an extremely important point for all women to understand: the tie that binds a man to a woman is *not great sex*; it's an emotional attachment that stems from his being able to foresee you being a great friend, true confidant, and future partner. If you sleep with him immediately, there is no time to establish any meaningful ties that will bind him to you. When it comes to sexual desire, men are driven by their instincts more than women are. Deep down inside, a vast majority of men still want to run through the streets of their town or city and sleep with as many women as possible in a twenty-four-hour period. When you sleep with a guy after three hours on your first date, by the time he is buttoning his jeans to leave in the middle of the night, he is already gearing up to run down the next street in search of his next conquest. Therefore, your immediate priority is to get to know and understand the guy sitting across from you while giving yourself to him in small, mysterious, and sexy doses. In summary, this is when you need to form an emotional attachment with him. The carrot of sex will keep him around long enough to become attached.

•••• ACT TWO: THE CONVERSATION ••••

 We constantly get complaints from women who tell us they have to carry the conversation whenever they go out on a date while the guy sits there answering questions. Sound familiar? If so, you may relate to the following true story.

A few years ago a young woman—we'll call her "Cathy"—came to us looking to be matched up. As always, we conducted an initial consultation with Cathy to make sure she understood the matchmaking process as well as her own expectations. She had recently moved to New York City from Chicago and found the dating scene in Manhattan to be very difficult to navigate. She was not into Internet dating. She preferred to meet new people while exploring her new city. Indeed, Cathy didn't have trouble meeting men to date. In fact, since she had arrived in New York City six months ago, she had been on a date almost every weekend. Given that, we were surprised that she was willing to pay a matchmaker to do a search for her. The problem, she said, was that guys never called her back for a second date. To find out more, Matt conducted what we call a "role reversal" with her on the second meeting. A role reversal is when Matt or I sit with clients and pretend we are on a date with them to see how they do. Within five minutes of the pretend date, Cathy had made every dating faux pas in the book. After those first five minutes the guy knew all of her dating history as well as all of her likes and dislikes. We realized that while she had mastered the art of meeting men, once she was out on a date with them, things quickly went downhill.

Cathy had what I call "reporter syndrome." She basically interrogated the men once she got them alone, and, inevitably, she scared them to death. She would question them immediately about whether they wanted to get married and have children. She'd probe them about past relationships, even going so far as to ask them how many people they had slept with! Within the first five minutes of date #1, she was asking date #5 questions.

When it comes to date #1 conversation, the key is to make it light. Don't act like a bubbly airhead, but do lose the seriousness. Men often tell us that women interview them on a first date—Barbara Walters style. When I heard this complaint, I realized this was what I had done for years. I thought I was being efficient. In my mind, I simply didn't want to waste my time, so I set out to find out exactly who the guy was, what he wanted, and where he had been in life—all on the first date. And I was good at it—remember, I'm an investigative reporter. These guys weren't getting anything past me! Looking back, I'm sure I scared plenty of guys away by grilling them like an FBI agent at what they thought was going to be a nice dinner with a nice girl. No wonder many of the guys I've gone on first dates with had a frightened look on their face even before we ordered our entrées!

To find out how the first-date conversation should go, read on. Matt and I have devised a foolproof first-date conversation guide so you won't feel like you are the halftime entertainment show or an investigative reporter trying to break the guy down until he opens up and confesses everything.

Topics Not to Discuss

 Let's start with my list of topics best left off the table lest he go running for the door before the main course arrives:

SEX. Women write to our website, Sassybean.com, all the time asking when is the best time to tell a guy how many men they have slept with. The answer: NEVER! No matter how many times he asks and how much he reveals about his own sexual history, past sexcapades have no place in your current relationship. If he is relentless, then use the "silencer." Simply ask him why he is so concerned. Is it because he is afraid that his performance will pale in comparison with the other men you have been intimate with? That should be enough to end the conversation. If it is a health concern on his part, tell him safe sex is part of your modus operandi and offer to produce test results. This is not a place where I feel full disclosure is the best policy. If you answer the question honestly, there is a chance he is not going to like what he hears. No number is the right number. Whether it's one or one hundred, it'll be the wrong answer because it just brings guys to a place they can't stand to be—picturing you with another man.

MARRIAGE. Do I even have to discuss this one? The only way a man will view a woman who speaks about getting married on a first date is as *desperate*. This is one emotion that men can smell a mile away. It is also the easiest way to turn a guy off. The best way to keep a guy interested is to act like one, when it comes to commitment anyway. So put thoughts of marriage out of your mind. When you are with him, live in the moment. Do not talk about the future in any way. Do not even talk about the next day. If you can maintain this "living in the moment" mentality, he will be the one to start talking about the future, and then you'll know you've got him!

THE PAST. Please remember your relationship past has nothing to do with your relationship present or future with Mr. Right Now. Please take all of the jaded relationship baggage and leave it at the lonely hearts terminal. Better yet, take all of the lessons you've learned from bad relationship experiences and apply them to more efficiently navigating your current relationship. Do not start a new relationship being skeptical, jaded, or negative. The gorgeous guy sitting at the bar with you doesn't care how it felt when you found your last boyfriend in bed with your sister. He won't feel sorry for you. He will most likely look at the situation from a stranger's perspective (because at this point that's what he is; it's only your first date). This information will be a turnoff to any guy.

HE'S RUNNING IF YOU TALK ABOUT . . .

- ✦ Therapy or rehab of any kind
- ✦ Babies: anything about them
- ✦ Love: the concept, the thought, or the premise
- ✦ Breakups: good, bad, or ugly
- ✦ Your girlfriends: he doesn't care, believe us
- ✦ Things you hate about your body
- ✦ Puppies, kittens, or any animal smaller than twenty-five pounds
- ✦ Zodiac signs
- ✦ Makeup, fashion, shoes, or nails
- ✦ All things related to that time of the month

HE'S LISTENING IF YOU TALK ABOUT . . .

- ✦ Things that turn girls on, but do not reveal any personal preferences
- ✦ The amount of private time you require. Make sure you say you need plenty!
- ✦ The HBO series "Entourage"
- ✦ Rational thought with an independent disposition

Conversation Rules

When it comes to first-date conversation, I have three simple rules.

RULE #1: BE A GOOD LISTENER. Women should not reveal too much about themselves too soon, no matter how comfortable they feel on the first date. Men have a hard time with emotional intimacy at any time in a relationship, so in the beginning, less is definitely more. And sadly, oftentimes, no matter the man or his maturity level, he is interested in two things on the first date: the way you look and whether he has a shot at taking you home.

Men also have extremely fragile egos, so be sure to make tons of eye contact and, for goodness' sakes, ask follow-up questions when he is pontificating about himself. If you let him take control of the conversation, it will make him feel like he is important and in control of the date. Your interest in what he is saying will put him at ease and allow him to drop his guard so you can start to see who this guy really is. But don't take this to mean that you should clam up. While you don't want to be overeager and spill the beans on your entire life or probe too hard, you do want the conversation to flow. There is nothing worse than awkward pauses or downright silence! Just be natural.

RULE #2: BE MYSTERIOUS. The guy doesn't want to hear about your last boyfriend, your last one-night stand, or the breakthrough therapy session you had yesterday. Too many women put it all out on the table. Not only do you run the risk of scaring the guy away, but you'll almost certainly bore him to death. Think of your life story as a season of "The Sopranos." If all the characters got whacked in the first episode, what would viewers have to look forward to for the rest of the season? Let a man work to find out who you are. Remember, men like a challenge. You can start sharing all your dirty little secrets later—or how about this idea: never!

RULE #3: BE UNIQUE.   Guys are not looking for the stereotypical woman from Singlesville. They don't want Carrie, Samantha, Miranda, or Charlotte. The traits these women possess, like partying, having one-night stands, and being dramatic, are all major turnoffs to men. Men actually like to see some stereotypical male characteristics in women. They like women who are not emotional, women who do not turn everything into season seven of "Sex and the City," and women who are not in constant need of reassurance. Stand out from the pack, and be unique.

ACT THREE: MINDIN' YOUR Ps & Qs

Believe it or not, guys want to be with a woman who has class. So, be sure you're on your best, most ladylike behavior during date #1. Here are a few tips on how to class up your act.

Two-Drink Limit

The main reason a guy asks you out is that he is incredibly attracted to you. If he is like a majority of men, he wants to sleep with you the first night you go out. You know it, I know it, and he definitely knows it. Mr. First Date doesn't have a whole lot of allegiance to you yet because he hardly knows you. So, unless he's a saint he will use anything to his advantage to get you into bed. And alcohol is his weapon of choice. Look, all guys, including myself, have had private conversations with waiters telling them to continue serving their dates their drink of choice until dessert. We do this for one reason: to get you into bed. To make sure you don't end up in the sack with Mr. First Date, just make sure you don't have more than two drinks. It's that simple. Here are two reasons that your two-drink minimum will pay off. One, it will set you apart from other girls he has gone out with. All of us guys have gone out with girls that have gotten hammered and gone home with us and had crazy, drunk sex. Yes, it's exciting, but we don't end up having relationships with these girls because in our minds, they've been categorized into girls who are easy. And the fact is that guys don't want to bring easy girls home to meet Mom and Dad. (I know it's a double standard because all guys are easy and don't get that rap, but like it or not, it's the way our minds work.) And two, a guy doesn't want a girl for a drinking partner. If you're guzzling beer and throwing back shots with your date, don't be surprised if he slaps you on the back and asks you what you think about the blonde at the other end of the bar.

Made to Order

 Restaurants are the most common dating venue. Dining out on a first date presents its own potential pitfalls. Nothing will ruin the look you've spent days putting together faster than a piece of spinach stuck in your teeth. Here is a list of first-date menu items to steer clear of.

✦ **Sushi:** It just can't be cut into small enough pieces to look delicate, so don't bother.

✦ **Soup:** Slurping can get ugly while you're giving someone that knowing look.

✦ **Bread:** No matter how small you break it, it can and will get stuck in your teeth. Plus it can make you feel bloated. Avoid it for the night.

✦ **Garlic:** Even if you have Altoids and mint sugarless gum, garlic is not the smartest option for a first-date dish.

✦ **Linguini or spaghetti:** It's sloppy and you don't want to be twisting things around a fork and hoping nothing falls on your shirt before it reaches your mouth.

✦ **On the side:** The fad diet of the moment may have to be put on hold for the first date. You don't want him to see you spend ten minutes trying to place an order with the waitress, putting things on the side, creating a meal that's not even on the menu, or sending something back because you taste a little butter in it. He will think you have either a serious weight problem or, worse, a serious mental problem. Try to order from the menu, deal with it if there is something you don't like, and don't complain about the food. It's a turnoff for the guy, and he could take it personally, especially if he picked the place.

Cell Off

Yes, we all have our cell phones because we want to stay connected to the world, but for the few hours that you're working to navigate your first date, leave your cell on vibrate in your purse. Nothing is worse than answering a cell phone during a date. If it is a work emergency, then you may excuse yourself, briefly, and take the call. But be sure to let him know it was work and not some guy you're meeting for a late-night dessert! Texting is another taboo for any date—not just the first date. He has no interest in looking at the top of your head while you text away on the cell phone on your lap. If it turns out that the date is a disaster and you need to send out an SOS text to one of your girlfriends so that she can call with an "emergency" phone call to get you out of it, excuse yourself to the ladies' room to make the call.

Leave Your Friends at Home

Matt and I had a client who was looking for a husband. We'll call her Ms. Social Scene. Ms. Social Scene went out all the time, but for some reason she never met the right men. She was pretty, young, and very much into "the scene about town." After a few weeks, her first match was chosen and she went out with a great-looking guy originally from England. We'll call him Big Ben. Big Ben was tall, handsome, a complete gentleman, and every bit as social as Ms. Social Scene. We believed it was going to be the perfect match. The location was set, and they agreed to meet at a rooftop bar in Manhattan's trendy Meatpacking District.

When it comes to our matchmaking clients getting in touch with us after their dates, the men and women are a bit different. Women usually call on their way home or once they get home from the date. But the men, well, the men can take days to call, if they call at all, to let us know how it went. We usually get our information from the women. This time was the exception. About two hours after Ms. Social Scene and Big Ben met up, Big Ben called my cell phone. When I saw his name come up on the phone, I knew he was going to tell me he was in love. Why else would he call? Maybe they were together and wanted to thank me because they hit it off right away! "Hey, buddy! Are you two having a good time?" I asked. To which Big Ben replied in a most ungentlemanly tone: "Was tonight a three-for-one date special, or did I just get lucky?" Confused, I asked, "What do you mean? Did Ms. Social Scene drink too much?" Big Ben replied, "No, actually she only had one drink, but the two friends she invited to meet us drank me under the bar. I spent three hundred dollars on drinks tonight on women I don't even know and don't care to know." I was shocked. Ms. Social Scene was definitely the girl about town, but I had no idea she would be bringing half the town on her date. When I called Ms. Social Scene to ask her why in the world she had brought her friends on the date, she said she thought it would be fun for Big Ben to meet her girlfriends, and the more the merrier, right? Wrong. The more the merrier doesn't apply on the first date. Men are not interested in buying your entourage drinks or dinner if they have asked you out. They want to get to know you, so give them the opportunity to do just that.

• • • • • • • • • • • • THE FINALE • • • • • • • • • • • •

Here are a few tips to follow to make sure you end the date on a high note.

Be the First to Say Goodnight

Dinner went so well, he even asked you to go to the famed Four Seasons Hotel for the sexiest dessert known to mankind—chocolate soufflé. The date could not have gone any better. He actually exceeded your expectations. So, what do you say to his invite? The answer is simple: you graciously decline, thank him for dinner, and tell him definitely some other time. Do not give him an explanation of why. In the beginning, you absolutely want to avoid being an open book. I know it sounds stupid to decline an invitation to have dessert with a guy you just had a great dinner with, but it's better in the long run to create mystery. Why take the chance of making a misstep and turning him off? So, stop the date while you're ahead of the game and leave him wanting more.

No Kissing, but You Can Touch

It's been a great date. He even took a cab back with you across town to make sure you got home safely with no intention of trying to get up into your apartment. As you get out of the cab, your heart is pounding, you want this guy so badly; but if you sleep with him this early in the game, you might not ever see him again. So what's the best move here? Make sure you take time to stop and thank him again for a great evening. Be sure that you are staring right into his baby blues or bedroom browns. Face him and stand no more than a hugging distance away. As you say good-bye, reach out for his hand. As he extends his hand, pull him in closer and whisper in his ear (with your lips brushing up against his cheek), "You're the sexiest boy I have been out with this week." Then smile, turn your back, and go into your apartment. This accomplishes two things: First, it makes the guy feel like you have other guys interested in you. This will make him see you as a hot commodity, thus making him want to compete and have you all to himself. Second, it strokes his ego but still keeps him in line by telling him that he was "better than all of the others, but not good enough to kiss—yet."

Zip It When It Comes to Future Communication

As mentioned before, don't talk about any type of future communication. Don't say, "See you around," "Look forward to talking," "E-mail me," "Text me," or "I would love to see you again." These are his lines. Remember, only think in terms of the present moment. Wait for him to be the one to initiate future plans. Say, "Good night, I had a great time," and leave it at that.

. . . .   **CURTAIN**   . . . .

The first date is your opportunity to show him what a star you are. Leave your stage fright at the door—there's no need to be nervous. It's your night to shine. But remember, you're not just putting on a show; you've got the goods to back it up! So, put your best self forward and we guarantee you'll leave him wishing for an encore!

7

DATING DISASTER SURVIVAL GUIDE

All dates are not perfect. In fact, some very ugly things can happen in the world of Singlesville. And while they may have absolutely nothing to do with you, you are forced to deal with them at least for the evening. As a result of some of the stories we have heard from our clients over the years, Tamsen and I have put together a survival guide for dating disasters. Hopefully, you will never have to deal with any of these sticky situations. But if disaster does strike, instead of stalking out of the restaurant, spending a week hibernating on the couch, or calling all of your girlfriends for confirmation that you reacted appropriately, deploy one of our foolproof damage control strategies.

DATING DISASTER #1: HE IS A NO-SHOW

Your hair is blown out, your manicure is shining, and your hip, hot Lucky 7 jeans zipped up without incident. You couldn't look or feel any better. As you run back and forth to the bathroom checking yourself in the mirror in disbelief at how perfectly you have put yourself together, you notice the time and start to feel a small twinge of nausea. You think to yourself, "He did say 8:00 P.M., right?" Questioning yourself, you pull out your Blackberry and double-check his e-mail: "Yep, there it is, 8:00 P.M." Then why is it 8:20, and you haven't heard from him? You then start a neurotic dialogue with yourself that goes like this:

"Oh my God, this isn't happening. I'm not being stood up. Of course I'm not! Traffic at this time can be a bear. He is probably running late. I'll just relax and not move so I will stay in this preserved state of perfection until he gets here. OK, what time is it now? It's 8:26. Jesus, if he is late, then why hasn't he called to tell me he is on his way? Calm down, jeez, maybe he's not a 'call if I'm running late' kind of guy, and he hardly knows me anyway, so what does he owe me? It's not like I'm sleeping with him! I could just call him and find out what the deal is. No, I'm not going to call him; that's desperate and pathetic! What time is it now? It's 8:40! OK, now I feel like I am going to throw up! I know, I'll call Stephanie and ask her what she thinks. . . . No answer. Oh God, I feel like the biggest loser on the planet!"

You continue this crazy conversation with yourself until 9:15 P.M., at which time you officially label Mr. Right as a no-show.

The first step you take in this situation is to erase all e-mails from Mr. No-Show along with his contact information, because obviously this is a deal breaker. There is absolutely no excuse for standing someone up. Look, it's not a perfect world.

Things come up and schedules change. So making a phone call to reschedule a date with advance notice is totally cool. We will even go out on a limb and say rescheduling a date at the last minute, with a phone call, because of an emergency situation, is still OK. But blatant disregard for another person's time and feelings is completely disrespectful. This is most likely a symptom of a much bigger problem this loser has. MOVE ON! And *do not* take it personally. His not showing up had nothing to do with you and everything to do with him!

DATING DISASTER #2:
HE BRINGS HIS BUDDIES ALONG

 You met him online, and after a few flirty exchanges you decide to meet up. He sounds mature enough, and his profile reads perfectly. Interests: sports, hanging out with friends, exploring the city, and traveling. "Perfect," you think to yourself, "maybe we have a match." The date is for 8:00 P.M., and you decide to show up on time because being fashionably late is out of style. When you arrive, you don't see anyone sitting at the bar alone, so you slide onto the nearest barstool and order yourself a glass of merlot. As you pretend to play with your phone, just in case he saddles into the empty seat beside you, someone taps you on the shoulder. "Hey, we are over here," says the someone. You're confused. You recognize his face, it's definitely your date, but who is this "we" he speaks of? As you look over his

shoulder, you see two other guys sitting at the table, and you realize he brought his buddies along. Now what?

As mature as some men can be, there are still many in the dating pool with the maturity level of young boys. Remember, men can be extremely insecure, and they seek approval from their friends. While it can be insulting or downright frustrating to a woman to have a bunch of friends along on the date, try to understand that he may just not feel like he has the ability to keep the conversation flowing on his own. Men also develop bolder personalities when their wingmen are in tow. At this point, most women would be annoyed, and some may even say to the guy, "I thought this was a date." Try to be a good sport (the first time), and wait until the second date to assess whether he is mentally ready to date a woman one-on-one. Without hesitation, say, "Oh my gosh, I didn't even see you guys over there. Let me grab my drink." Act as if you're not flustered in any way.

When you reach the table, smile, say "hello" to each one of them, and pretend you have three dates for the evening. In this case, you don't have any obligation to be focused solely on him, even if you want to be. If he is testing you to see your reaction to his friends, you just passed the test. Do not act angry, annoyed, pouty, or irritated. Make yourself enjoy the evening, even if you are disappointed deep down inside—the worst that can happen is you have a great meal, have some good (or at least decent) company to share it with, or have weeded out another frog hiding among the princes. When the evening is over, make sure you leave alone and tell each one of the guys you had a great time. If he is a real man, your date will be calling, and this time he will want to take you out alone. Whether you let him will be up to you. This scenario is not necessarily a deal breaker, despite the fact that it can make for a rather disappointing evening out. You should try to give this guy a second chance. Ironically, he may have been trying to make a good impression on you by showing you his "bolder" personality with his friends by his side. But a word of warning, if date #2 includes his posse, there is to be no date #3.

DATING DISASTER #3: HE TELLS YOU HE FORGOT HIS WALLET

The restaurant he picked is perfect, especially since you didn't even think you were having dinner. When you made the date, it was just going to be drinks, but the food smelled so good that you bypassed the bar and grabbed a table in the corner. He is funny, talkative, and such an improvement over the other guys that you have been striking out with over the past few months. Then the check arrives. If you feel so inclined, in a rather obligatory way, you can touch the top of your purse as if to say, "I am an independent woman and am not looking for a free ride." But you don't hear the words from this date that usually follow the "go into the purse" move: "No, please, this is my pleasure." Instead, you hear, "Hey, thanks for getting this one. I forgot my wallet."

This is a tough one for the independent, modern women of today. On one hand, you don't want to act as if you expect the guy to pay, but on the other hand, this *is* a first date, *he* asked you out, and, quite frankly, you didn't even plan on eating. With that, you pay the check, and he sits there as if nothing is wrong. But, there is something wrong with this scenario, and it has less to do with you now being a hundred dollars in the hole, and more to do with his carefree attitude about the fact that you just took him to dinner. Men don't forget their wallets. And if they do, they do something about it, like call a friend to bring it to them, arrange with the waiter to bring the money back later, or pay you back the minute you get home. If a man thinks he can enjoy your presence through the evening and then skip out on the check, he is sadly mistaken. In a case like this, unfortunately you are left with little choice but to pay the bill and try to act classy about it. If he is testing you, you don't want to see this joker again. If he doesn't have the money, he shouldn't have asked you out in the first place, or he should have come up with a less expensive plan. Sorry to sound harsh, but if you are footing the bill now, wait until there are real expenses in the future.

A little side note about picking up the tab. The women I work with in Manhattan do and should expect the men to pay, and there is nothing wrong with that. In fact, I tell all of the men that I send out with my female clients that they must always pick up the bill. No exceptions. But I know plenty of men who actually get insulted when a woman just sits there and expects the guy to pay. These are not real men in my opinion, but they are out there living among us and you have to be equipped to deal with them. If you go out with a guy and he's visibly annoyed that he is expected to pick up the tab, then be relieved; he has just saved you time and weeded himself out. Guys should pick up the tab, at least for the first few dates. After all, how much dinero did you drop on hair, makeup, wardrobe, pluckings, and waxings!

DATING DISASTER #4: YOU
•••• BUMP INTO YOUR EX-BOYFRIEND ••••
WITH HIS NEW GIRLFRIEND

 It's been exactly six months since Mr. X ripped your heart out of your chest and made you feel as if you could never love again. After a long summer of watching "Sex and the City" reruns and crying whenever Mr. Big hurt Carrie, you finally muster up the courage to say yes to going out on a date. The guy is someone who has asked you out before, but until now you just couldn't even think about another guy without bursting into tears over Mr. X. Your friends are tired of your dwelling on him, and finally they stage an intervention with ice cream and *When Harry Met Sally*. As a result, you realize that it's time to get back out there, so you get all gussied up and prepare for the doorbell to ring.

When your date arrives, you realize he is kind of cute. He has a sort of European look, and you have always had a thing for men with dark hair and blue eyes; maybe tonight won't be so bad after all. With that, you both set out for the evening. He informs you that there is a new restaurant he has been dying to try, so he made reservations about a week earlier. You think to yourself, "Mr. X never bothered to make reservations in advance," and you are excited about the evening. When you get out of the car, he runs around to open your door, a perfect gentleman, and with that you proceed into the restaurant, only to find yourself face-to-face with your Mr. X, who is on his way out the door with his new girlfriend. What do you do?

As your heart races, and you feel like you are going to throw up the meal you haven't even eaten yet, you must act as though you are in total control. This is one of the hardest situations you will ever find yourself in. You must say "hello," take the initiative to reach around him to his girlfriend and extend your hand, and then make sure you *immediately* introduce your date. Do not stand there with your eyes brimming over with tears. Do not stalk past them both and "accidentally" knock shoulders with her. And last, do not pretend that you don't see them. After you have said "hello," *move on.* No need to make small talk, ask where she is from, or worse, say something you will regret. Act as if he is a friend, and don't let your date know that this is the man who kept you holed up in your house for six months. After you have handled the situation with class and courage, you will be able to have a nice evening. Despite the fact that you probably will want to cry, deep down, know that you are an amazing person for how you acted, and that Mr. X is the one missing out.

DATING DISASTER #5: HIS EX IS THE BARTENDER

You are not a big bar person, but you agree to meet him at what he called his "favorite local haunt." You dress casually in a pair of jeans and sling backs and a cute baby-doll T-shirt to give off the air that you care but not too much. When you arrive at the bar, it's a little trendier than you thought it would be, and it definitely doesn't feel like a "favorite haunt"; rather, it is a little haughty. The bartenders are dressed in cutoff tops, the music is blaring, and there is little chance of a decent conversation. Nevertheless, you decide to be positive. After all, he approached you at Starbucks; he must be interested.

As you scan the bar, you notice him sitting there looking a little annoyed, but since you are not late, you figure it doesn't have anything to do with you, so you sit down next to him and smile as if to say, don't worry, I'm not the kind of girl who would keep you waiting. But something doesn't seem right, and before long you realize that this is his favorite local haunt because the ex he was madly in love with is one of those haughty little bartenders. You know this because in a very bitter tone he casually mentions it to you after she takes your drink order. He asked you there to make her jealous! Do you act flattered? Is it a compliment that he thought you would make her jealous? Or do you get angry because this is clearly a waste of your time?

In a case like this, you get to feel both ways. The best thing to do is to not take it out on either one of them. Be gracious; accept your drink without giving her the evil eye or him the cold shoulder. This is definitely an uncomfortable situation, but you can make the best of it. Try to be understanding; we have all been there, hurt by someone and hoping to make him or her jealous with a new person. Unfortunately, you are the pawn in this case when you just wanted to have a good night with a nice guy. Best advice: finish your drink, then tell him thank you and that you have an early morning. While it may sound abrupt to leave after fifteen minutes, he is lucky you stayed that long. This won't require an explanation, and if it does, be frank by telling him you would be happy to see him again (if you still want to after this), but it will have to be in your neck of the woods because his woods are too crowded.

DATING DISASTER #6: HE ••• STARTS CRYING AT DINNER ABOUT ••• HIS EX WHO DUMPED HIM

So, you swore off all hot, hunky players and dedicated yourself to finding a guy who has substance. You were looking for some emotional depth and intelligence. Thus, when Steve, an editor from your

Japanese cooking class, pulled you aside and asked you out to dinner, you accepted and looked forward to a date with a guy who had feelings rather than abs. You don't know much about Steve except that he is nothing like the usual no-substance, model-like guys you have wasted your time on in the past. He is educated, serious, and seems to be "artsy." Yes, artsy; you can't believe that adjective can be used to describe someone that you are about to go on a date with.

On the night of your date, you meet Steve at a cute BYOB in your neighborhood. He is waiting at the table with a great bottle of French wine. In the middle of his explanation about the origin of the wine it hits you how refreshing it is to listen to an educated man speak as opposed to blocking out third-grade rhetoric being spewed from a gorgeous idiot across the table. Yes, intelligent Steve might be a keeper.

Then, all of a sudden, you think you hear the words *ex-girlfriend*, *romantic vacation*, *broken heart*, and *still in love*. Your reverie is broken, and you rush to make sense of what he is saying. Steve has just told you that the wine reminded him of a romantic vacation he had taken with his ex-girlfriend to France, where she broke his heart. He also said that he thinks he may still be in love with her. Steve then proceeds to bury his head in his hands and start bawling like a two-year-old.

Obviously, you need to tell yourself this is not a movie or a dream. This is reality, and you are here with a real person, and men like this actually do exist. At this point, all sexual attraction, romantic feelings, and genuine interest in Steve have evacuated your body. So, this is easy: be his friend and help him out. Try to explain to him that he is not ready for dating, and he needs to heal. Tell him that you will be his friend and there are many other girls out there who won't break his heart. You, on the other hand, need to get to a trendy bar with a group of your girlfriends to look for a hunk with some brains. They do exist; just be patient and don't settle.

DATING DISASTER #7:
• • • • • • HE TELLS YOU HE DIDN'T • • • • • •
REALIZE YOU WERE SO OLD

The following is a true story; the names have been changed to protect the innocent and the idiot. Michelle was a forty-three-year-old office manager of a law firm. She was an average-looking woman who had taken a beating from the New York City dating scene. She retained my services because she did not have the energy to go out and find "the one." She told me that she was looking for "just a normal guy" who was around her age and open to a serious relationship. It was actually refreshing to hear a woman who had realistic expectations regarding her dating requirements. So, I began my match selection process. I chose David, a forty-two-year-old attorney from the Upper West Side. I felt David was a great match for Michelle because he was her male equivalent in many ways. He was average in appearance and was looking for a woman between thirty-five and forty-two years of age. He was sick of women in their twenties who didn't know what they wanted, and he was ready for a more mature woman that he was attracted to and could have a worthwhile conversation with. When I told him about Michelle, he seemed to be interested in meeting her. He asked how old she was, and I told him she was around his age, but I didn't have her folder in front of me. I went on to remind him that he wanted a woman that had substance and was more his equal as opposed to arm candy. He agreed to the date.

I still remember the piercing ring of my Blackberry at 8:20 P.M. the night of their date. Caller ID told me it was Michelle, and the time told me there was a chance the date was a disaster. The voice on the other end of the phone was one of controlled rage. Michelle's opening line was, "Matt, are you aware that I just paid you to set me up with a guy that looked straight into my eyes and told me that I was too old for him? He then proceeded to point to a gentleman who had to be at least sixty years old and tell me that he looked like someone I should be dating. Then he got up, threw twenty dollars on the bar, and left." This was probably one of the first times in my life that I have actually been rendered speechless. I mean, what do you say to something like that? Michelle then proceeded to lambaste me over David's behavior. I said that I was sorry and that I had no idea how any man on this earth could ever treat a woman so disrespectfully. I told her she would be a lifetime member of Matt's Little Black Book. (Six months ago, after several more *good* dates, Michelle moved in with a man I introduced her to. I'm waiting for my invite to the wedding.)

If you are ever in a situation like this one, we don't have to tell you it's a deal breaker. There is no being polite. There is no reason to worry about what he thinks. And there is no apology accepted. Get up, walk out, and move on. If you give it a second of thought after that, it's too much time wasted. This may be easier said than done, but trust me, it's not worth your time to even give it one tear or one conversation afterward.

DATING DISASTER #8: HE GETS DRUNK AND ACTS LIKE A FOOL

The drinks just keep coming, and before long you realize that your date is completely and utterly drunk. "How could this have happened?" you wonder. You asked him to your friend's dinner party because he was such a dream on the first two dates, and now this?

Now what? On one hand, you can subscribe to the theory that boys will be boys. On the other hand, you don't want a boy; you want a man. If your Mr. Wonderful has gone overboard with his intake of rum and Coke, it's time to take him home for the evening (his home) and leave him there. This is probably not what you want to hear, but I am a firm believer in setting boundaries early on in a relationship. Getting drunk and acting like a fool in front of your friends is a dating deal breaker. If he has too much to drink, that's one thing; acting foolish and pawing your best friend in front of her fiancé in a drunken haze is quite another.

DATING DISASTER #9: HE TALKS ABOUT SEX ALL NIGHT LONG

There is nothing wrong with feeling like he wants to rip your clothes off, but when he can't stop talking about it, the turn-on changes to a turnoff. You are wearing the hot little wraparound top that makes you look like a size-C cup despite the fact you have been struggling with a B cup average most of your adult life. When you enter the bar, it's noisy and crowded, but in no time you spot your date. He is actually a little cuter when he isn't in workout clothes, and you mentally pat yourself on the back for looking so good. As you sit down, the standard round of volleying questions back and forth begins: So, where are you actually from? Do you have brothers and sisters? How long have you been at your job?

After the typical *ohs* and *ahs*, the conversation suddenly takes a very different turn, and now the game has heated up. He asks, "Have you ever had sex in a public place?" Alarmed, you try to do the girl giggle to get out of answering the question, wondering if he is serious. Suddenly you realize he is serious, so you say, "Have you?" He answers yes and proceeds with the line of questioning. What do you do? Do you go along with it so you don't seem like a prude or tell him you are offended and stalk out of the place? You need to let him know, in a very polite way, that you don't have a problem talking about sex, but you do have a problem discussing it before you have had a chance to find out what he does for a living. You can be classy and change the subject, and if he doesn't get the hint, put your hand on his arm and gently say, "You will find out all you need to when it's time." If he gets it, perhaps there is a chance of a second date. If he doesn't, and his sexual fantasies continue to come pouring out of his mouth, it may be time to down that drink and head on down the road. He is clearly interested in one thing, and he ain't getting it from you on date #1.

DATING DISASTER #10: HE ADMITS HE IS MARRIED

For this scenario I'm going to draw from my own experiences. I was in my dating prime and always happy to go to a great lunch or dinner with a guy just to get a better sense of what kind of mate I was actually looking for. I was narrowing down my list of "What I Want in a Guy" and almost had it perfect. Unfortunately, nothing prepared me for the next date I was about to go on. I was covering a political event, and a guy, who was the lead singer of the salsa band playing at the event, kept looking over at me. He was not necessarily cute, but he was definitely charming and of course very entertaining. But I was working and didn't have time for someone who was trying to get in front of the camera. When the band took a break, he came over and introduced himself, handing me a card. When I looked down, I saw the letters *JD* after his name. "You're an attorney?" I asked him. "Yes," he replied. "I love to sing, and since I can't pay the bills with my singing, I practice law during the day, so I can do this at night." I was impressed to say the least, threw his card in my bag, and didn't think much more about it. Two days later, an assistant to Mr. Salsa called with him on the line. I was shocked when she put him through. I had never given him my phone number, but he apparently saw where I worked and took the initiative (or at least his secretary did) to locate me. He asked me out to lunch for the following week and I accepted, not thinking anything of it.

A few days before we were scheduled to go out, he left the address of the restaurant on my machine; I knew the place, but not very well, since it was totally out of the way and in a weird location. I met him there the following week. He had a table in the back, and I mean the very back corner, and the place was practically empty. When I sat down he was a totally well-mannered gentleman. He ordered me a drink, and we got to talking. About halfway through the meal, we started talking about our upbringings, families, and so forth, and without warning he pulled out his wallet and showed me two photographs of the most beautiful little girls I had ever seen. "Nieces?" I asked. "No, they are my daughters," he replied. Alarmed, I tried not to act surprised, so I said, "Oh, do they look like your ex-wife?" I was even less prepared for his next remark. Casually, very casually, he replied, "I am not divorced. My wife and I see other people. My daughters, though, are my life. My loyalty lies with them; that's why I will never leave her."

Although I'm a woman of many words, I was speechless. Without saying another word, I finished my lunch. Then, when he asked about dessert, I said to him: "Mr. Salsa, while you are being a loyal father to your daughters, I am going to be a loyal person to your wife." In one move, I grabbed my purse and left the restaurant as he called out after me. Mr. Salsa called my phone about twenty times over the course of the next two weeks. I never responded.

I hope by sharing my experience I have given you some insight into how you should respond if you are ever faced with a bold, married man who thinks he can play on the singles field. You don't have to be classy about your exit, just make sure you make one. If you are in public, leave. If you are in private, ask him to leave. If he calls, do not answer. And if you start feeling yourself weaken, call a friend for some tough love. Mr. Married is bad news. Don't let a dating disaster become a life disaster.

It's impossible to make it out of Singlesville unscathed. But these dating survival strategies will ensure that you get out with your dignity and self-respect intact. Plus, being armed with the knowledge that you can handle any dating dilemma that could arise will give you tremendous comfort and confidence as you embark on your search for Mr. Right. So, keep your chin up and hope for the best, and remember, if you end up sitting across the table from the worst, you'll know exactly what to do.

8

WHY HASN'T HE CALLED?

You just closed your door behind you; the date is over. It went exactly as you dreamed it would. His eyes practically popped out of his head when he saw your outfit. The restaurant he chose was perfect, and the conversation was effortless. He was a gentleman and, quite frankly, looked even cuter than when you met him at the park. He cleaned up rather nicely. You slip off your shoes, check your machine, and start thinking about what a great night you had. Sometimes Singlesville, and first dates especially, can be quite depressing but not tonight. Tonight you're on cloud nine. You can't wait for him to call; after all, he said he would.

Indeed, when the night ended, he squeezed your hand, gently gave you an innocent peck on the cheek, and said, "I'll give you a call." But it's now been two days since your "perfect date," and the only messages on your voice mail have been from your mom and the dentist's office confirming your next appointment. You can't concentrate at work, food has no taste, and your favorite show has gone from riveting to annoying. You feel anxious, and for the thousandth time you shut your eyes and grit your teeth thinking: *"Why hasn't he called?!"*

Men don't call for several reasons. They are not all good reasons, and with some men there is more than one. In this chapter, Tamsen and I will provide insights into why he hasn't called as well as a few good reasons to be relieved if he hasn't. Then, we will offer solutions and suggestions on how to get the next guy to call.

• • • • • HE DIDN'T CALL BECAUSE . . . • • • • •

Here are a few reasons why he didn't pick up the phone and dial your number.

You Are Not His Priority

You're familiar with the thoughts and expectations of a woman after what she thought was the perfect date. Now, we'll let you in on the thoughts of the guy she went out with that same night. We'll call him "Dave."

Dave's phone is ringing as he enters his apartment and flips on the light. He answers the phone, and on the other end is his best friend.

Friend: *"Yo, Davo, you get laid?"*

Dave: *"No, no, man, she isn't like that."*

Friend: *"C'mon, man, you couldn't get laid in a morgue."*

Dave: *"Look, dude, she's a cool girl! She's got a killer body and a little bit of smarts, so she ain't layin' down that easy."*

Friend: *"Are you going to go out with her again?"*

Dave: *"Easy, man, I just got home. I haven't even thought about it. I might give her a call next week. But as you know, I gotta deal with trying to end it with 'Freakshow Caroline,' stop booty-calling Donna, and try to get through two sales presentations this week. But with that ass this new chick's got on her and that cute smile, I will do my best to hook up with her."*

Friend: *"Cool, you hear about the game?"*

Notice, just as quickly as the conversation about the date started, it ended, and at that point the guy has moved on to a new topic. The only thing you need to take from this seemingly silly interaction with his friend is that Dave, while he had a good time on the date and thought the woman was "cool," did not immediately go home and start analyzing the date. And he certainly wasn't concerned about what was going to happen next. Dave was on the date. It ended. He had a good time, and without hesitation, he mentally moved on to something else.

THE TOTEM POLE THEORY.   When it comes to women, or anything else for that matter, men compartmentalize. Let me explain using a theory of mine that I call the Totem Pole Theory. All men have a subconscious totem pole that dictates what they will give their attention to at any given time.

In other words, the key parts of a man's life are ranked in a certain order of importance, and where you sit on his totem pole depends on several things, including his availability, his attraction to you, your behavior, and, above all, timing. When it comes to timing, there can be several factors at play: Is he ready for a girlfriend? Is he happy with his career? Did he just get out of a terrible relationship? Is he about to move to the other coast?

According to my Totem Pole Theory, this is usually the order of his priorities, even after you have had a first date with him:

1. His career
2. His friends
3. The girl he is currently sleeping with (don't be naïve)
4. His dog
5. You

You are the low man, or in this case woman, on the totem pole, but this is not something to be offended by. When you enter a guy's life, it already has multiple moving parts, just as yours should. You have to be patient and allow him to put you where he thinks you fit. But take heart: you do have a bit of control over your placement. Ultimately, it will be determined by the way you conduct yourself during the initial stages of your relationship. Forcing yourself on him, putting pressure on him, and constantly making yourself available will result in a low placement (somewhere around where his pet fits into his life). Patience, independence, and always being a challenge to him will get you into first position. You may not be his priority at the moment, and as a matter of fact, you really shouldn't be! Keep your ego in check! He has not yet discovered that you are the end all and be all. Give him a chance to realize how just amazing you are.

Additionally, be aware of guys who move women up the totem pole solely based on their appearance. These guys tend to lose interest quickly. Also watch out for the guy who drops everything and moves a woman up the totem pole after a first date—if this happens, you better run. This is a warning sign of a dependent, needy man. The best relationships are the ones where it takes you a little while to get up the pole. (Yes, I said "pole"; please keep your mind out of the gutter!)

Because He IS into You

Do you remember the little boy who sat behind you in first grade and used to yank your pigtails? Well, this is the guy you just went out with, except he no longer sits behind you, and you're no longer sporting pigtails. Now the way the dynamic plays out is like this: you went out on a date with him, he likes you, and he is nervous about calling you because he is into you. This guy is easy to read. He had a great time, but he is trying to practice the so-called three-day rule, so he is forcing himself not to call you.

The three-day rule applies even more with a guy you have gone out with than it does with a guy who has just taken your number. Give him a chance, even if he doesn't call after three days; if he is into you, he will. This guy is just trying not to show his cards so that he doesn't get his heart trampled. He doesn't want to come across as too needy by calling you too soon. You have your strategy, he has his.

To Him a Call Equals Commitment

As the woman, you are only looking for a second date in that phone call, but for a man, that call often means he is getting himself further obligated to seeing you. After the call he'll start spending time with you, calling, texting, e-mailing, and before he knows it, he's committed to you, a family, children, dogs, houseplants, a lawn mower, and . . . and the list goes on and on and on in a man's mind. Sounds crazy, but it's the truth. This is how a man processes a simple phone call early in the courtship. While a man wants to call you for a second date in hopes of getting another step closer to sleeping with you, he's aware that you may misinterpret the call as him wanting to commit. A commitment can be a frightening proposition if a man isn't ready—yet another area where men and women differ. The male mind tends to remember all the negative things from past relationships, whereas the female mind remembers the positives. When you have a great first date with a guy and he can visualize you as a potential candidate for a serious relationship down the road, all the stakes suddenly become higher in his mind. This is what takes place.

When a guy starts to see characteristics in you that allow him to see you as his future partner, he then subconsciously applies all of his past negative relationship experiences to his current situation. If he is not too frightened, he will eventually make the phone call. But if he is not calling because he believes that a call will quickly

His Positive Observations	His Fears
1. You Are Independent	1. I love the fact that she is not the clingy type. She would be the perfect girlfriend. But, I've been tricked by this before. First she is so independent, and then as soon as I get together with her, she probably won't leave my apartment.
2. You Are Not a Party Girl	2. My mother would love this girl. She actually cooks! Who cooks these days? Oh no, why am I thinking about her meeting my mother? I swore that I wouldn't introduce any more women to my mom. I don't need that headache again, after what happened with my ex. They still talk on the phone; it weirds me out.
3. You Didn't Sleep with Him	3. I want to sleep with her so bad; she is so sexy. But I'm scared she will turn me down. On the other hand, I don't want to offend her by not calling. I want to see her again. Wait, what am I saying? If I see her again, she'll want to see more of me, and before I know it we'll be picking out wallpaper at Home Depot. My last girlfriend tried to trap me into that.

equal a giant step toward a committed relationship, then you have to give him a "cooling off" period to realize that his positive observations outweigh his fears from past relationships. This is not easy. In fact, it is probably the most difficult thing you will have to do. Our advice: BE PATIENT, do not panic, and do not call everyone you know trying to get their assessment of *your* situation. This is one of those things that will take a little bit of time, so use the time to make sure of what *you* want, if you plan to move forward from this point.

He Thinks You Don't Want Him To

 Yes, you read it right; he hasn't called because he thinks you don't want him to! Surprised? Don't be, because it's more common than women realize. There are three types of women that men don't call back because they think you don't want to be called. If any of these descriptions sound familiar, maybe it's time to reassess the vibes you're sending out.

LITTLE MISS INDEPENDENT. It's a first date. The man and woman are getting to know one another, and at the next table a little boy screams out that he hates his food. The woman says, "Children are unsanitary, and quite frankly I have no interest in having any spawn." Although this may be true, to a man it is a rather startling statement because men subconsciously visualize all women wanting two children and a minivan. Although we know this is not always the case, the conclusion is that the woman on the date is not interested in children, a man, or anything else that would stand in her way of a kick-ass career and doing exactly what she wants to do when she wants to do it. Little Miss Independent comes across as a high-energy, no-strings-attached woman who couldn't care less about a man, marriage, children, or a future. It may or may not be true, but either way, if this is what a man perceives, it is the truth as far as he is concerned.

THE MAN HATER.   The Man Hater is a woman who has dated extensively, has turned bitter, and is overly anxious to find a partner. But instead of acting needy and loving and nice to be around, she acts like the mortal enemy of the male gender. Man Haters often bring up past relationships, blaming their ex for the relationships' failures. Man Haters enjoy hanging out with other Man Haters and ripping on the male species. And Man Haters are never, ever happy. Whether they're sitting at the local diner or are on a jet headed to Paris, nothing is ever good enough because they're not happy with themselves, and therefore no man will ever satisfy them. Man Haters don't get second dates.

MISS PEDESTAL.   Miss Pedestal acts so far above the man that he believes, right off the bat, that she is not interested in him. In this case, the women have usually come out of rather unsatisfying relationships and have vowed that they will never make poor choices again when it comes to choosing men. Miss Pedestal puts herself above everyone and expects to be treated like no other woman, forcing a man to jump through hoops just for a first date, and it doesn't stop there. She is very open about her expectations: where she wants to live, how she wants to live, and what she will and will not accept in life. Miss Pedestal's life is similar to that of a confirmed bachelor in that she is not flexible and willing to change her lifestyle for a man or anyone else for that matter. In the case of Miss Pedestal, her expectations are unrealistic, and all men, no matter who they are, will fall short. Miss Pedestal has put herself above the fray, and she will remain there alone.

He Has Man-Child Syndrome

 Man-child syndrome means that a man is a sixteen-year-old trapped in the body of a forty-year-old; therefore, his dating behavior is that of a teenager. Man-child syndrome is a common condition striking even the most successful of men. Because of his lack of maturity, any adult behavior, such as calling a woman after a terrific evening, makes him uncomfortable.

One of my clients' dating experiences describes classic man-child syndrome behavior: This particular client was a lovely young woman who came to me looking for dating advice after going on a disheartening date with a cute guy in her building. She kept running into the guy, and finally he asked her to hang out one weekend. On the night of their date, they ended up at one of the hottest spots in Manhattan. The guys were hot, and the girls all looked like models. My client could definitely hold her own, so I was surprised this bothered her. But as her story unfolded I came to understand why. She said at one point she went to the ladies' room and came back to find another woman sitting on *her* barstool talking to *her* date! The guy seemed completely oblivious and never asked the woman to get up; in fact, he introduced them and continued talking to the beautiful girl who was perched on my client's stool.

After another fifteen minutes a third woman joined the group, and the man went on to give that woman as much, if not more, of his attention. When my client finally told him she was leaving, he replied only that he would see her around. When it comes to dealing with someone who has man-child syndrome, you must be the adult. You cannot sit there and go along with his immature behavior. In fact, you need to make it perfectly clear that it's unacceptable. And you must be willing to accept the fact that he may not grow up anytime in the near future, giving you no choice but to leave him in his sandbox with the other kids while you go look for a grownup to date.

He Is a Confirmed Bachelor

 A confirmed bachelor is different from a player. Although they have very similar characteristics, a confirmed bachelor can be even more frustrating to a woman because he doesn't even pretend. He lets the woman know she'll have a great time with him in the present, but there is no hope for a future together. He is not settling down, ever. When he talks about the future, he uses the word *I*, not *we*. If a man is a confirmed bachelor, he will not, under any circumstances, call within a week of the date, and the most skilled confirmed bachelor will give it about ten days. He hasn't called because he knows if he does, he will have to ask you out again and more than just casual dating will be expected of him. For a confirmed bachelor, time is a luxury, and he has plenty of it because he has no plans to settle down. If the guy you went out with doesn't call or waits ten days to pick up the phone, chances are he is a confirmed bachelor. My advice: lose him.

You Called Him First

The minute you dial his number after the first date, you have just showed him all of your cards and given up control. I'm not exaggerating. Think about it. When you pick up the phone and call him, you are setting the parameters of the relationship, if you even have a chance at one after this move. You will always be the person who decides the time and place, takes charge of your dates, and acts like the man in the relationship. If you call a guy to tell him you had a great time, or worse, "just to see what's up," he will think one of a few things:

+ That you need to be in control
+ That you are desperate
+ That you are going to smother him if he asks you out again

If you initiate a call after your first date, that will give him enough of a reason not to ask you out for a second date. So, don't pick up that phone, e-mail, or "just send him a short text." You have made it perfectly clear that you are interested; if he doesn't return the gesture, you need to return to the land of dating and look for someone else to go out with.

You Are Not for Him

There were no signs that he wasn't going to call. You didn't see any red flags, and in fact *he said he would call.* So, why has your phone been more silent than a monastery of monks? The hard truth is that it takes time to find a perfect fit. The reason he doesn't think you're a fit for him could be attributed to a thousand different things, from the color of your hair to the sound of your voice to your inability to feed his inflated ego. The fact of the matter is you are simply not for him and never will be. This does *not* mean that there is anything wrong with you. And it may not mean there is anything wrong with him. There is no solution to the problem in this case because there isn't necessarily a problem; you're simply not for him.

All men don't have to fall in love with you. The right one will come along, and he'll love your looks and the sound of your voice, and hopefully, he won't have an ego that needs inflating. This guy will never stop calling. So don't spend days checking his profile online or trying to run into him at the gym where you met. You went out, had a good time, and it's over. There is nothing more to do except stop waiting for him to call. You have more important things to do!

NO CALL, NOW WHAT?

If he doesn't call you after a week and a half, it is safe to say he probably won't. *This is OK.* This means that you just avoided a serious time waster in your life. The time waster is a man who is just not interested in you for one of the previously mentioned reasons. Ten days is ample time to handle any emergency, get his priorities in order, or even ask you out again if he is a confirmed bachelor. MOVE ON. Sure, it'll sting, but just a little. The man is not going to call, and if he does after a month or two, he wants sex. Let it go, and in the meantime take care of yourself.

✦ **Do not talk about him or try to analyze what went wrong.** Ten days was enough time to waste on wondering if a man is going to call you for a second date.

✦ **Accept that his not calling had *nothing to do with you.*** You are still the Bond Girl that ten other guys are waiting to meet.

✦ **Go out on another date as quickly as possible.** When your attention is focused on several men, you don't have time to worry about just one. But don't fret, when the right one does enter your life, you will be able to give him your undivided attention.

✦ **Add up the hours you have just wasted obsessing over this guy and spend the equivalent amount of time in the**

gym working out. Nothing can boost your confidence like working out; plus, exercise will fill your head with endorphins, those little chemical spurts that make you feel good.

✦ **Fall in love, with yourself.** There is nothing like spending some time alone, not thinking about anyone but you. Go shopping, hang out with friends, get a makeover, read a book. Do whatever makes you happy—you don't need a man to be in love.

HE CALLED; NOW WHAT?!

It's been more than five days. You are too exhausted to check your voice mail on your cell phone one more time. Suddenly, you hear an unfamiliar sound coming from your purse. You realize your cell phone is actually ringing. You answer the phone, and it's him! Steady girl, the first phone call after the first date can be tricky. Here are a few don'ts and dos:

When He Finally Calls, DON'T
✦ Mention the amount of time that has passed since your last date
✦ Ask him what he's been doing all week
✦ Tell him how happy you are to hear his voice

✦ Give him any attitude or make any snide remarks

✦ Stay on the phone longer than five minutes

When He Finally Calls, DO

✦ Act pleasant and be nice to talk to

✦ Let him lead the conversation

✦ After he's had a chance to talk, bring up a fun follow-up topic from the first date; ask how a project he mentioned went at work, about his best friend's wedding, or how his dog Fido is doing

✦ Casually mention how crazy your week has been (no details)

✦ Let him know you have things to do and have to run, but you look forward to the next date

Now, it's time to get ready for your next date. Here is a rough script for date #2.

✦ **Your role:** The only character you should play is yourself. He called you because he is interested in seeing you again and learning more about you. This means he wants to go out with the same woman he was with on the first date. So don't switch roles. It will make him second-guess why he picked up the phone if you were a lady the first night and decide to act the drunk party girl on the next date. Trust me on this one; otherwise the credits will start rolling before you can order dessert.

✦ **Wardrobe:** Be a little more daring with what you wear for the second date. You made his eyes pop out of his head the first night; now it's time to make his head spin. Highlight your best physical features, and give him some special effects he will never forget.

✦ **The cliff-hanger:** Do not get physical too fast. Just because he called doesn't mean you "owe" him anything. Go out and have a great time, but don't get all lovey-dovey on him and start making your second date a tell-all monologue about how you were hoping he would call. Let him tune in for a third date to learn how everything plays out.

9

IN THE BEDROOM . . . AND THE MORNING AFTER

Your dates have been perfect. On the second and third dates he was a complete gentleman. He wined you, he dined you; it was the best! The fourth and fifth dates were a bit more relaxed. One night you took in a movie, and the next day, you met his sister at brunch! Plus, he hasn't even tried to sleep with you. Well, he did try, but he didn't push it when you told him that it was still too soon. He calls when he says he's going to call, and he always shows up on time. Where did this Prince Charming come from? You must make him yours.

After sitting at brunch looking over at his sister, picturing the many shopping outings the two of you will have together once she becomes your new BFF, you become convinced that he is not a player, and you are ready to sleep with him. The last four dates ended with some heavy, heavy petting. It took every ounce of willpower you had to tell him it was time to call it a night. You have officially been seeing each other for seven weeks, and you feel like it's time to introduce him to the bedroom.

Sex. Is it time?

This is a tricky question, and there really is no right or wrong answer. Every person and every couple is different. But if a man has stolen your heart, and you think you are ready to sleep with him, make double sure that you are doing it for the right reasons. Make sure you're not going to have sex with him to keep him or to further the commitment.

There are some right reasons to decide to add sex to the relationship, but you have to make sure you are not assuming this will make you his girlfriend, bring him closer to you, or convince him to stop seeing other people. If he is currently still seeing other women or has been up front about the fact that he is not looking for a commitment, having sex with him will not land you a ring anytime soon.

Men don't think of sex in the same way women do. For men, it is a physical act that is in the moment; for women, it is an emotional act and an expression of how they feel about the man. The fact is you shouldn't have any expectations after you sleep with a man. That's right: no expectations. It is also not a good idea to sleep with a man just because you believe it's the next step in the relationship. Before you jump in the sack, make sure you understand the relationship you have with him and are happy with it. You must also be aware that sex changes everything. The morning after your first night together, you may feel closer to him or it may be the beginning of the end.

If you're simply looking for a bed buddy, then you don't have to worry about whether he stays or goes the next day, but if you're looking for something more, make sure you know where things stand.

This brings me to my next point: if you are trying to decide whether to sleep with a guy, asking him where he stands could be detrimental. Most men don't like to quantify their feelings or discuss and analyze the relationship. Remember, we're the great communicators; they're the ones who are great with directions and setting up the DVD player. The fact is many men don't know how to articulate how they feel. If you force the issue, more often than not you won't get a genuine sense of where he stands from his garbled attempt to "share his feelings." What you can do is observe his behavior to make sure you're both in the same place in the courtship/relationship. If you're not, sex isn't going to put you on the same page. In fact, if you add sex to the relationship for all the wrong reasons, you could put the kibosh on the whole thing. The table on page 180 shows some clues that will tell you what page he's on.

• • • • • • • • BETWEEN THE SHEETS • • • • • • • •

 So you've decided to kick things up a notch and have sex with him. Now what? How about a peek inside the male mind to get a better understanding of his thoughts when it comes to the first time he is going

He is interested in you if . . .

✦ he calls when he says he will and doesn't cancel dates.

✦ he takes you out to dinners, movies, and so forth, and spends time making plans.

✦ he books you in advance. He understands you're not a last-minute kind of girl. And he makes sure he sees you at least twice a week.

✦ he takes no for an answer when it comes to sex. He understands that you will when the time is right for you.

He is only interested in getting you naked if . . .

✦ he doesn't spend much time planning your dates or tons of money on them. He will go wherever you want and doesn't mind staying home.

✦ you've only seen him twice in the last three weeks, and he text messages you at the last minute to see if you are free for the night.

✦ he calls sporadically and only when there is nothing else going on.

✦ when you said you weren't ready to sleep with him, he left your house in a huff muttering the word "tease" under his breath.

to sleep with a woman he is genuinely interested in. Believe it or not, he is just as concerned about the big event as you are; take a look:

"OK, it looks like this is definitely going to happen. Good thing, because I really wasn't up for another night of takin' care of myself. In fact, this is the longest amount of time I have ever waited to sleep with a girl—either I'm losing my touch or she's something special. Either way I'm definitely looking forward to this!

"It's been a long time since I've had sex. I've been putting so much time into making this happen that all my booty calls have gone by the wayside! But thanks to my patience, I'm at risk of performing like a high school boy. Being a 'preemie' the first night with a girl is so not right. What can I do before we hit the bedroom to make sure I don't lose it too soon? Maybe I could run to the bathroom and take care of myself before we go at it. . . . No, that's just too weird! OK, I need to just calm down and think. . . . Damn!

"I know, I'll use my patented 'hold her hands above her head' move. This usually works in a situation like this. By taking both her wrists and holding them above her head (with one hand, further proving masculine dominance) I can take care of two things at once. Without the use of her hands she won't be able to stimulate me to the point of becoming a teenager. And it'll allow me to work that beautiful body of hers without her giving me directions. Do I hate that!"

You've probably gathered that his primary concern is his performance in the sack. Men are preoccupied with thoughts of how they will measure up and how the woman will rate their performance. You, on the other hand, are more worried about how your body is perceived by a man, how it compares with the other women he has slept with, and what he's thinking and feeling. Knowing exactly where a guy is coming from in this situation, and how his perspective differs from yours, gives you an advantage: not for game playing, but so you can be understanding and avoid making missteps before, during, and after sex.

In summary, it's up to you to decide when it's the right time to sleep with a guy. But since you get to control *when* it takes place, how about letting us control *what* is taking place (the first time, anyway). Read on for some pointers on how you can help him believe he's in control the first time the two of you have sex.

MATT'S "FIRST TIME" SECRETS OF THE BEDROOM

Take these insights to heart to ensure a successful first round.

No Drunk Girls Allowed

You went out and tossed back a few too many cosmopolitans, and you finally worked up the nerve to sleep with him. But

if you're staggering to the bedroom, having a difficult time seeing him clearly, and can't figure out how to take off your dress, save it for another night. Men don't like sloppy, drunk women who are giving them slobbery kisses and are not really aware of what's going on. If you have had a few too many, instead of sleeping with him, sleep it off.

Silence Is Golden

Talking about the relationship in bed can turn a man off faster than a cold shower. This is not to say that you are supposed to be meek, boring, and submissive—there's nothing wrong with a little lighthearted dirty talk (but don't overdo it the first go-around, lest you freak him out). Do be yourself; just make sure you do not use this time to discuss your feelings or where things stand in the relationship. When you are horizontal is not the appropriate moment to ask him the question that evokes fear and dread in even the strongest of men: "What are you thinking?" If you must know, here is your answer: he is only thinking about how great it is going to be!

No Instructions, Please

Don't tell us what to do; the last thing we want to hear are instructions on how to best turn you on. We know you know your own bodies, we know you have "toys" that work better than we do sometimes, and we know your last boyfriend wore a size-13 shoe, but we don't need a reminder the first time we sleep with you. Please, no instructions during sex if it's your first time. Don't worry, after the first time, we'll be asking you for pointers!

Pornlike Behavior Is for the Movies

Screaming, screeching, and animated behavior is not as big a turn-on as the "pros" make it out to be. Just be natural when you're between the sheets. Men who are really into you are not looking to be entertained or convinced that you are really turned on. Relax, enjoy yourself, and respond when it's natural, not on cue.

Hold the Laughter

You are so excited and giddy, and happy that the night is finally here, that you belt out a giggle while he is sliding out of his boxers. Bad move. REALLY BAD MOVE. A man doesn't want to hear any laughter when he knows he is being sized up for the first time. Cut him a break, try to keep your emotional high to yourself, and don't give him the lowdown on your emotional state at that moment. Let him concentrate on you and enjoy the night, not wonder how he is measuring up to the last man in your life.

Give Up Control

For women who are independent, have conquered the business world, and are in charge all day long in their lives, this is often a very difficult thing to hear. But as a man who is privy to what men say behind closed doors and whisper to each other when there are no females around, I can tell you men want to be in control (or at least think they are in control) during the physical act of sex, at first. This is not to say that once you have a sexual relationship you should just do nothing, but the first few times, a man does not want to be manhandled, thrown around, and made to believe he is not in charge. Let him believe he is—at first, anyway—even though we all know that is often far from the case!

Three's a Crowd

If you want to kill the mood in record time, mention your ex or, worse, his. Men don't want any reminders of the past when they are about to get intimate with you. Don't ask for reassurance that he feels the same way about you that he did about his ex-girlfriend or tell him that you slept with him sooner than you did the last guy you fell between the sheets with.

Don't Say "I Love You"

If you are going to exchange "I love yous" for the first time, it should not be when you're horizontal. Men are controlled by passion and are all wrapped up in the heat of the moment when they are in bed with you, so if you say "I love you," and he responds in kind, you have no way of knowing whether he really feels that way or if he's giving you an obligatory response so he can get on with the act. If you are going to say "I love you" (you shouldn't be saying this first, but that's another book), wait until you're both vertical, you're both sober, and you're prepared for his response.

Put Your Toys Away

Men are not interested in seeing your toy chest the first time you have sex with them. Put your toys away. We don't want to compete with gadgets that run on batteries and move in ways that no man ever could. In time you can certainly throw in a toy or two to jazz things up. Just not at the beginning.

Don't Ask Him to Stay

Most men will have enough respect for you and for the night of intimacy that you just shared to stay the night. But if for some reason you get what we call a "bolter," let him go. A bolter is a man who cannot wait to run out the door so he can sleep alone. But don't misunderstand his rush; it's not because he's not interested in you. In fact, it's about him, not you. Men often have to confirm that they're not going to lose their independence after sleeping with you. They want to believe that they are still footloose and fancy-free even though they may be falling for you. Let him believe this fairytale and he will want to stay the next time around. The more you pull a man to be with you, the harder he'll push you away.

TURN HIM ON FROM HEAD TO TOE

At Sassybean.com we randomly polled one hundred men to find out what *keeps* a man turned on in the bedroom. Here's what the guys have to say! (Notice, many of these turn-ons were turnoffs the first go-round; it's amazing what a little confidence building will do.)

✦ Smell. Whether you're wearing La Pearla, Vicki Secrets, or his tighty whities and a baby tee, men are going to be turned on by you, but your smell is the real tell-all. Men love

(continued)

the smell of a freshly showered woman with clean hair and a little dab of perfume at the nape of her neck.

✦ **Skin.** Guys say that skin is in. On the list of turn-ons, soft skin against their bodies was a must.

✦ **Women who take charge.** Men like nothing better than to be the one to just lie there on their backs and enjoy your aggressive sexual moves. But wait until he has had a chance to be in control a few times. You don't want to set a precedent that you'll forever be the boss between the sheets—trust me, you'll want your fair share of takin' it easy and letting him do all the work.

✦ **Toys.** Once you've had sex enough so that you feel comfortable together, pick your favorite toy and introduce it to your favorite man.

✦ **Foreplay.** Don't let your love life fall by the wayside once you get into a relationship. Keep the foreplay alive. It will bring you both to the edge and keep him coming back for more.

✦ **Adventure.** Men love to be taught new things and be taken on adventures, especially in the bedroom. Once you are both comfortable with each other, anything goes!

✦ **Your mouth.** It's sexy and sensual, so pucker up!

✦ **Feet.** Polished toes are a must. In fact, make getting a pedicure part of your regular routine.

✦ **No hair.** Hairless everywhere—it's not the seventies.

✦ **Good breath.** Minty fresh.

••• IF HE DOESN'T WANT TO HAVE SEX •••

 We have been telling you all along that men are only after one thing in the beginning. But what about the ever-elusive man who is not ready for sex or not really interested in it at all? First of all there could be a laundry list of reasons a man is not interested in sex. Let's start at the top.

He Is Sleeping with Someone Else

This is never an easy one to hear, but if you are trying to get a man into bed and he continues refusing your advances, he may be having his fun elsewhere. If this is the case, this guy is uninterested in anything physical and will always find a rather flimsy excuse for going home early or falling asleep before you can even climb into bed. You are probably wondering why he would even go out with you to begin with. Well, chances are he would like to be with you but hasn't made a clean break from the person he's with, either because he isn't brave enough or because he isn't ready. It is important for you to try to get to the bottom of this so that you are not yo-yoing back and forth trying to figure out if you are doing something wrong. If you do realize that he is still sleeping with someone else and is not yet willing to let that relationship go, you need to let him go so he can figure out what he wants and not waste your time.

He Is Freaked Out

Women are not the only ones who get a little nervous before sex. Men also feel enormous pressure. Deep down inside, he wants to make sure he doesn't suck in the bedroom. You will not find a plethora of men willing to fess up to this, but it's true. If he is comparing himself to your ex, had a bad ending with his, or just feels intimidated by you, he could take a little longer to warm up to the idea of sleeping with you.

Arm Candy Anonymous

He takes you *everywhere!* You have met all of his friends and his parents adore you, but for some reason, after a great night out, you go home alone. Every time. Face it, lady, this guy is a member of "Arm Candy Anonymous." In other words, you are there for show-and-tell for him to impress the folks and his friends. He has no intention of being with you long term. While he may be "sweet" to you, if you detect that this erratic behavior is going on for too long, it could be time to find a new man to spend Saturday night with.

It is also possible that he has someone else on the side whom he thinks his friends wouldn't accept because perhaps she is not attractive enough. It's also possible that he's not interested in women at all and is just not ready or willing to reveal that to the people in his life. There's not much you can do about either of these points, so if you suspect this is the case, it is probably time to move on.

• • • • • • • • • • THE MORNING AFTER • • • • • • • • •

The morning after is actually more important than the night of. Allow me to explain. The night went just as you had planned. It was perfect. He had all the right moves. And you weren't so bad yourself, Miss Thing! Luckily, it all came back to you. Just like riding a bicycle, as the old cliché goes. Afterward, you drift off to a sound sleep thinking about the glorious life you'll share together. But before that glorious shared life comes "the morning after," which can be not so glorious and rather uncomfortable. Picture it: Morning. The sun comes streaming in through the open blinds. As you try to focus, you wonder who in the hell left the blinds open. Suddenly you realize you don't have blinds, and this is not your bedroom. As you bolt upright in bed, memories of last night come rushing back to you. Last night was the first time you had sex with Mr. Prince Charming, and just as you start flashing back through the highlights, he walks through the doorway with two steaming lattes (or at the very

least instant coffee with some Coffee-mate thrown in), a sexy smile, and those piercing baby blues. Suddenly, you are over-come by the realization that this man could be "the one." Now what? Should you tell him you love him? Admit last night was the best sex of your life? Or go back to sleep and hope he never asks you to leave? The answer: None of the above. As always, you have to think a few steps ahead of him. You must avoid becoming the "static clinger" who won't leave his apartment. Stick to the etiquette I've outlined below and your life will be full of mornings after.

✦ **Do not linger.** Drink that foamy, tall latte (or horrifying instant coffee), grab your bag, and head for the door. This isn't being rude, it's being smart. You're a busy woman with places to be, so get moving. The same course of action applies if he spent the night at your place. Men are not like women. After sex they're not looking for affirmation that you still like them, so don't slowly run your fingers over his comforter, tell him you love goose down, and ask him to come back to bed and snuggle. Throw off the covers, get out of bed, go brush your teeth, get your clothes on, and get out of there. Think about it: it's the first time you've slept together, and he has no idea what to expect of you. So, take this opportunity to impress him with your coolness. Sure, he had a great time, but he could be a little nervous that he's now entering the "relationship zone." Don't make him feel like sex with you means by next week you will be picking out china patterns. Let him know that you're an independent woman who enjoyed the evening but now has to move on with her day. If he wants you to go and grab breakfast, politely decline and tell him you would love to, but you'll have to give him a rain check. He'll be so impressed with your cool, independent attitude that he'll be calling to cash that rain check in before too long.

✦ **Do not mark your territory.** Do not treat his house like your dog treats a fire hydrant. Yes, you finally slept with him. But this does not give you a free pass to mark your territory to make sure that other women know you were there. This means you do not leave earrings, ponytail holders, or your lipstick-stained water bottle on his nightstand in case some other woman or his ex stops by for a visit. Take it all with you when you go. And you should never ask him if you can "just leave this T-shirt, toothbrush, or comb." Do not assume you are ever coming back. This is not to say that you won't, but if the night was as special to him as it was to you, you will be back, and in time you will have a drawer to leave things in, and before long you will graduate to the closet. In the meantime, he doesn't need subtle reminders that you were in his bed. If he doesn't remember having sex with you, a ponytail holder will do little to bring back any erotic thoughts of you.

✦ **Save the snooping for another time.** Listen, I'm not going to pretend the minute a guy I was with walked out of the room I didn't go flying through his drawers to find out what deep, dark secret he was trying to hide. I've been there. In the closet, in the drawers, I even went through the cell phone of a guy (or two) to find out what he was trying to hide. If you do what my friends and I refer to as "the check," save it for another time. Can you imagine rummaging through his nightstand drawer just to look up and realize he was watching you for ten minutes in the doorway after your first night together? Save it, or stop it altogether. If you have such a lack of trust, maybe you shouldn't have slept with him to begin with. But, since you did, save "the check" for another time!

✦ **Don't ask, don't tell.** As you are making your morning-after exit, don't ask him if he's going to call you, and don't tell him what a beautiful night you had in his arms. This is a must. In this case, you must assume he had a beautiful night just as you did and that he is going to call like he has been all along. If you ask him, "Are you going to give me a call later?" I can almost guarantee he won't. Or if he does, it won't be because he wants to; it will be because you made him feel obligated with your question. And if you tell him that it was the best sex of your life and you have never felt this way before, he'll run for his life. Men are like horses—they spook easily. It's important that he doesn't feel trapped now that he's slept with you. Make sure he knows that things will remain the same. Yes, you've been intimate, and now you both feel a bit closer to one another, but that doesn't mean you're to start closing in on his life just because the relationship has progressed.

✦ **Use your minutes for someone else.** Don't call him, he'll call you. Again, if you start smothering him, making him think you are going to start calling every five minutes and cannot live without him, you may quickly find yourself solo. Call a friend, call your mom, I don't care if you call your ex-boyfriend (as long as there isn't anything between the two of you), just don't call him. Let him miss you and track you down.

✦ **Keep your mouth shut.** This is probably the toughest one of all. There is nothing wrong with telling your best friend or your sister about the awesome night you had, but leave it at that. Don't go calling people you haven't spoken to in six months to let them know you are in love, or phoning mutual friends to tell them it "finally happened." Be respectful of the night you had together. Plus, you don't want it to get back to him that you couldn't wait to brag about your sexcapade. It will make him think you didn't take it that seriously and that perhaps you don't really care about him like he thought you did.

•••••• AFTER THE MORNING AFTER ••••••

 Sex can bring two people closer than anything else in the world. Sex can also make a relationship so confusing that it brings a bond to a screeching halt without warning. It is no mystery that a woman is usually

GETTING YOUR LOOK RIGHT
BETWEEN THE SHEETS

What's his favorite look between the sheets? Should you slide into bed wearing sexy lingerie, boxers, or nothing at all?

✦ **The Businessman:** His bedtime fantasy girl is worth millions. If this is your man, he prefers an upscale, sexy look that classically highlights your curvy body. He is a true gentleman who appreciates all the accoutrements that dress up your bedtime look. Lace up a beautiful corset with detachable garters and a matching G-string. Make sure those sexy, satin stilettos match your bedtime attire. And when the closing bell rings, leave the heels on.

✦ **The Jock:** He's simple, sweet, and oh so sexy! It doesn't take a lot to make this hunk happy. Less is more, so follow the rules in his playbook and you will be sure to score. Any baby-doll tee with cotton panties will surely make you his MVP (Most Valuable Princess). Just in case his rippling biceps aren't enough to keep you warm, put on a pair of low-waisted pajama bottoms and a skintight shirt to show off that beautiful body of yours. He will be sure to keep the stadium lights on in order to see your every move.

✦ **The Bad Boy:** This bad boy has a mission when the lights go down, so he will need to be entertained but kept in line. He has no desire for you to "slip into something more comfortable." G-strings, thongs, and bikinis should fill your lingerie drawer. Other options: boy shorts and a see-through tank top. By the end of the night, you will definitely be the one laying down the law.

✦ **The Prep:** An Ivy League look will graduate you to the top of the class. Your man loves the wrapping on the present almost as much as the gift itself. Conservative, cute, and sexy, that's what will sail his yacht. The top must match the bottom in this case. So, slip into some cotton pajamas that highlight your curves, a T-shirt and boxer combo for hot summer nights, or if he is really in the mood, make him crazy with a classic lace bra and panty set.

✦ **The Artist:** Just as Picasso painted the "Girl Before a Mirror," your artist sees you as a vision of beauty. He is cultured, creative, and innovative. This art lover will appreciate your feminine form as it is meant to be—nude—in between the sheets. So don't go spending big bucks.

in control in terms of when things happen in the bedroom, but you must use this control wisely, and you must be fair about it. In other words, don't use sex as a weapon; it's often one of the most detrimental mistakes women make when they are trying to move the relationship to the next level. If you have decided to sleep with him, but then six weeks later you are still not sure that he is seeing only you or is interested in anything long term, don't use sex to figure out where he is coming from. Be honest with yourself and honest with him. If you aren't, at least one of you is going to get hurt. Here are some reasons *not* to sleep with your man of the moment, if you are serious about him:

+ Just because he wants to
+ Because he will pout and be frustrated if you don't
+ Because he calls you a tease
+ Because he says it will strengthen the bond that you already have
+ Because you feel it will make the relationship move to the next level
+ Because he says he loves you (and it comes out of nowhere)
+ Because you haven't had sex in a while and you believe you can do it without emotion
+ Because you want to get him away from the other women he is seeing
+ So he will start to look at you more like a girlfriend than a friend
+ Because you feel guilty

Just like any other "first" in a new relationship, the first time you have sex is a big step. What sets it apart from other firsts, however, is that it's one event that will definitely alter the relationship, for better or for worse. But not to worry, now you're armed with tried-and-true advice on how to handle this delicate relationship milestone in a way that ensures that you land on top! (Sorry, couldn't resist.)

COMMITMENT AND OTHER "C" WORDS

It's been exactly twelve weeks since your first date. You have seen him every single weekend. In fact, all weekend plans lately are completely assumed. He has seen you without makeup. He has experienced you with the worst case of PMS ever. And he even tucked you in and acted like a perfect gentleman when you had way too much to drink the first night you went out and partied with his friends.

And guess what? He's still around!

You are in a relationship—but is he Mr. Right? Women can spend years in the wrong relationship only to discover that he isn't "the one." A woman usually reaches this conclusion after figuring out that although he can commit to dating, he isn't willing to commit to a lifetime. On the flip side, you might be the one hesitant to commit, while he is madly in love and ready to say "I do!"

But let's focus on what you do know: he now calls when he says he is going to and you are no longer asking, *"Why hasn't he called?"* Instead you're asking, *"Where is this going?"* Once you get into a full-fledged relationship, this question seems to haunt you day in and day out whether you're in love, in lust, or just in like. In this final chapter, we'll take a look at the three Cs that must be considered in every new relationship: "Convenience," "Confusion," and "Commitment." Is it a relationship of convenience? Why all the confusion? Is there a commitment in your future? Addressing the three Cs will ultimately help you figure out if he's Mr. Right or Mr. Wrong.

• • • • • • • • • • • • CONVENIENCE • • • • • • • • • • • •

 Ah, the man of convenience. As girls we often have a hard time admitting that we are in a relationship of convenience rather than passionate, fairytale true love. All of us girls are looking for that white knight to come galloping along, sweep us up onto his horse, and protect us from the big, bad world for the rest of our lives. The problem is your white knight's means of transport is a white '99 Toyota Corolla instead of a white horse, and instead of sweeping you off your feet, he mostly just comes over and watches TV. As for protecting you, you have a security alarm, a dog, and a big bottle of mace, so that's not really necessary.

But the relationship does have a few redeeming qualities. The sex is great. And he's a nice guy. In fact, he is one of the few nice guys left in Singlesville. So, do you stay or do you go? You don't really want to break it off with him right now, but you're not sure you want to be the princess in *his* castle (or studio apartment, as the case may be).

So, what's a girl to do?

Here's my advice. Before making your decision, take a look at the pros and cons of a relationship of convenience. The pros: you have someone to hang out with on Saturday nights, and you have a date for major events such as weddings, graduations, and Sunday night dinner at your parents' house. And he's fun to be with and much cuter than any of the other guys you've been out with lately. Plus, he's head-over-heels in love with you, worships the ground you walk on, and is willing to do anything to see you smile.

Now, let's examine the cons. Although the sex is great, you have little to talk about outside the bedroom. His idea of a great Saturday night is renting a movie and cuddling in front of the television instead of going out to dinner with the many fun couples you know. And he won't stop talking about the future, which really puts you in freak-out mode.

Now consider these important points. It's not necessarily a bad thing to be with a man of convenience; it really just depends on where you are in your life. Maybe you're busy with your job or taking care of elderly parents. If you're busy and he is just someone to pass the time with, it may not be so bad to continue the relationship as is. But it could prove to be a serious time waster for the both of you if you're not honest with him about where you stand. A man of convenience is just that—convenient for the here and now, but not likely to be in your future in five years. If he fits into your life and you are not really searching for true love, have a great time and enjoy yourself in the here and now. But, if you're hoping to get married in the near future and ultimately want someone to spend your life with, a man of convenience is taking away precious seconds that you can't afford to waste.

• • • • • • • • • • • • CONFUSION • • • • • • • • • • • • •

 If you find yourself stuck in a relationship cycle with a guy who's constantly breaking up with you, only to reconsider a week later and beg for you back, it's important that you take a step back to get a sense of what's really going on. If a guy is giving you mixed messages,

wanting you one day then dumping you the next, he's most likely caught up in his own confused state. He can't decide whether he wants a committed relationship with someone he has a real bond with or if he wants to be back on the field again where he can do as he pleases with whomever he pleases and not have to answer to anyone. You must take stock of what's going on because your time is too valuable to waste on Mr. Confused. Let's take a quick peek inside the confused mind so you can get a better understanding of what I mean.

The second a guy feels as though he's in a relationship he involuntarily short-circuits. Take a look at what's going on in his head: The guy, we'll call him "Peter," has just dropped off his girlfriend and is driving home on his Harley. As he stops at the light, a gorgeous girl crossing the street looks at him, winks, and says, "Nice bike!" "Oh my God," Peter thinks, "that girl is on fire. I'm going to pull over as soon as the light changes and get her number. I better motion to her to meet me across the street." He motions and she complies. "Damn! What am I doing? Shelia [his girlfriend] would kill me if she found out. On the other hand, what Shelia doesn't know won't hurt her, so what the hell. But how am I going to pull this off? I have plans with Shelia all weekend, and we talk every other hour! God, I never thought about it, but that's way too much! Why should I blow this opportunity to pick up this hot chick? It's not like I'm married or engaged or anything. Screw it, I'm pulling over." He then flips on his turn signal and starts to slow down. "God, look at that body! Wait a second, that's my phone vibrating. Damn! Shelia's calling, what timing! I have to take this call." Peter turns off his turn signal, waves at the girl, and accelerates home. "I can't believe I just completely blew off that gorgeous woman! It sucks to feel this way. Maybe Sheila isn't the one for me after all. I'm starting to resent that she calls me her boyfriend. Not a good sign. Might be time to have another 'talk' with her."

Meanwhile, back at her apartment Shelia is wondering why Peter dropped her off in such a hurry and wouldn't spend the night. They just had sex for the first time three weeks ago, and already he's acting bored with the relationship. This week he went out twice with his friends. It seems the minute they get close, Peter pulls away and wants to break things off. But then a few days later, he regrets his decision and starts calling again.

Sheila has every reason to feel confused. Peter is giving off tons of mixed messages. Men do reach a point in their lives where they start to value a true connection with a woman. The connection becomes more intellectual and more emotionally based than physical. Many men reach a point where this con- nection is so important to them that they are no longer willing to jeopardize it for a temporary, physical connection with someone they don't even know. But as you witnessed above, Peter completely got thrown off the relationship course by a hot girl on the street. For him, the confines and sexual limitations of being in a relationship became too much. It's a sad fact that some men can be so easily spooked out of a relationship by a beautiful girl they can no longer have.

If you find yourself in a relationship with someone like Peter where you're constantly breaking up and getting back together, it's safe to assume that one or both of you isn't ready to commit. Don't let yourself be a revolving door for a guy. Don't waste your time on a guy who can't figure out what he wants.

But for some couples, it does take a breakup to bring them closer together. The time apart gives them a chance to step back and look at the relationship with clarity instead of emotion. If each of you is honestly committed to making the changes necessary to make the relationship work, things will be much better the second time around. Just be sure you don't get back together because it's too hard being single. Be honest with each other and talk about how you both felt when you were apart. Give the relationship time to redevelop. It may be the real thing—or you could be postponing the inevitable. Here are ten signs to look for that may mean he's not the one:

1. **He is not a man of his word.** This means he says he is doing one thing, and later you find out he has done another. Trust is critical to a good relationship.

2. **You are not his priority.** Friends, work, his dog, his computer are all still above you on the totem pole. If you never made your way to the highest rung of the pole, he may not be the one.

3. **His past is present.** He can't give up talking to his ex-girlfriend. He has long conversations with her, brings up her name often, and compares you to her every now and then.

4. **He is selfish.** When he is given the choice of spending time with you or his friends, his friends win out. He wants to see you when it's convenient for him.

5. **He says he doesn't want to get married.** If the guy you are seeing says he is not ever going to walk down the aisle, don't think you are going to change him. While it may sound harsh, he most likely just doesn't want to walk down the aisle with you. So, start running the other way.

6. **He has cheated on you.** He can apologize, say it was the first time, or beg for forgiveness. But if a man has cheated on you, that is a pretty sure sign he is not the one. If you do decide to stay and give him a second chance, make sure you are prepared for him to do it again.

7. **He is verbally abusive.** If this man is critical of your every move, you shouldn't stay. Verbal abuse is not acceptable no matter how much you love someone.

8. **He doesn't respect you.** When you are in front of friends, he doesn't show any respect for your feelings or you in general. He is quick to jump down your throat and put you in your place. This is not the man for you.

9. **He criticizes your body.** Whenever you walk around the house in your sweats, he has something sarcastic to say about your body; you're either too fat or too thin. He is constantly comparing you to other women and makes it obvious he doesn't like the way you look.

10. **He is a womanizer.** You are at dinner trying to pick out what you are going to order, and instead of helping you decide, this guy is flirting with the waitress as if he is out with her instead. This man is not ready to settle down, and he may never be.

• • • • • • • • • • • COMMITMENT • • • • • • • • • • • •

He is doing all of the right things. He calls when he says he's going to call, and you have a great time when you're together. Does this mean he is the one? This question is so hard for women to answer because they don't want to waste any time with a guy who doesn't have the same future plan as they do. But women make the mistake of pressing the issue and demanding an answer regarding what the guy's long-term plan is for the relationship. The second a woman does this, she completely destroys any hope for a long-term relationship. As soon as a relationship is labeled, it takes on a whole different meaning to a man. The dynamic of the relationship changes in the male mind. A new set of adjectives starts to become associated with the relationship: *expectant*, *predictable*, and *consistent* replace *surprising*, *mysterious*, and *erratic*. When this occurs, men tend to run in the opposite direction. So, to make sure your commitment is real and will last, men need to initially feel a sense of "healthy doubt."

I define "healthy doubt" as a feeling that women themselves create in men through their own independent behavior. If a woman appears to care little about a long-term relationship with the guy she is dating, then that guy will start to question his worth, need, and value to that woman. He will then do anything to create a position of permanence in the relationship. So, never, under any circumstances, make an initial move to label the relationship or ask for a commitment. Below are ten signs that will help you determine he is the one, so you don't ever have to ask him.

1. **He understands.** He always tries to see your side of things. This means that even if he has seen you get upset or cry about

something a hundred times before, he still tries to calm you down and make you feel better.

2. **He tells you.** Oh those three special words, the words some men have major trouble saying. Well, if he says them often, count yourself lucky. Hearing him say "I love you," and knowing he means every word, is proof that he's the one.

3. **He shows you.** We all know most men have trouble expressing their feelings with words. Your man may use other forms of expression to let you know he loves you, such as taking you out for dinner when he thinks you need a break from cooking or understanding that you might need some time to yourself. While you may like to hear those sweet whispers of affection from him, just remember that actions speak louder than words.

4. **He listens to you.** Is he genuinely interested in what you're saying when you talk to him? Does he give you his undivided attention during your conversations, instead of having the television blaring in the background? It's an important sign if he shows he's really concerned about your feelings, and especially what you have to say.

5. **He's happy around you.** Smiles? Laughter? Excitement to be spending time with you and not his guy friends? If he can't get enough of you, it's a sure sign that he's really attracted and in love.

6. **He compliments you.** He notices when you change something about your appearance. He appreciates when you take the time to look great. When he looks you up and down admiringly with a little smile and tells you how beautiful you are, you know you matter.

7. **He appreciates you.** Telling you how proud he is of your achievements or praising you to his family and friends is a wonderful signal.

8. **He asks for your opinion.** He asks for your advice, considers it, and may put it to good use. When important decisions are at stake concerning him, he doesn't just go ahead and decide on his own what he thinks is the right course.

9. **He's interested in what you want, too.** Let's say you're both watching television and you want to watch "Desperate Housewives" while he'd like to catch "24." You know how men are when it comes to the remote control! If he lets you watch your show of choice, not in a grudging manner but because he wants you to be happy, you've got a winner. Give him extra points if he actually sits through it with you!

10. **He makes you feel special.** Finally, is he the kind of guy who's always trying to keep the romance alive? Bringing you flowers or breakfast in bed are both really wonderful ways to show he cares. If he's always going out of his way to make you feel exceptional, hold on tight—the man is a keeper.

JUST FOR FUN: THE LOVE TEST: IS HE THE ONE?

1. On my birthday and holidays my boyfriend's usual gift is . . .

   a. a beautiful piece of jewelry
   b. a seductive night of dinner and dancing
   c. a box of chocolates and a sweet card
   d. a text saying he won't be there

2. During our lovemaking he whispers into my ear such "sweet nothings" as . . .

   a. "I love you"
   b. "Babe, you are the one I've always dreamed of"
   c. "You drive me wild, your body is so amazing"
   d. "Can you go get me a beer?"

3. My guy and I go together like . . .

   a. peanut butter and jelly
   b. Brad and Angelina
   c. Batman and Robin
   d. Boston Red Sox fans and New York Yankees fans

4. Real love means supporting my man's . . .

   a. hopes and dreams
   b. decisions, even if I might disagree sometimes
   c. hobbies, even though they might not always include me
   d. unhealthy affection for Carmen Electra

(continued)

5. My boyfriend's favorite thing to text to me is . . .

   a. "I miss you!"
   b. "Wish I was there with you now instead of working late at the office"
   c. "I can't stop thinking about last night!"
   d. "This isn't working for me anymore"

6. My boyfriend's idea of a romantic getaway is . . .

   a. a trip to a secluded tropical island
   b. a weekend in Paris
   c. a surprise jaunt to his house in the country for evenings by the fireplace
   d. a night in jail for disorderly conduct

7. The movie title that best describes our relationship is . . .

   a. *Love Story*
   b. *Modern Romance*
   c. *Runaway Bride*
   d. *A Nightmare on Elm Street*

8. My boyfriend is most like this dog:

   a. a loyal St. Bernard
   b. a lovable yellow Lab
   c. a powerful German shepherd
   d. an angry little Chihuahua

9. If my man cooks me a meal, it's usually . . .

   a. a sensuous Italian feast
   b. champagne and oysters
   c. an egg-white omelet and fresh veggies
   d. Dominos double pepperoni with extra cheese

10. Our song is . . .

    a. "Endless Love" by Diana Ross

    b. "All You Need Is Love" by the Beatles

    c. "Ain't No Other Man" by Christina Aguilera

    d. "Love Stinks" by the J. Geils Band

YOUR SCORE:

Lots of As: YOU GO, GIRL! Your boyfriend is a keeper and really loves you! Consider him "the one"!

Lots of Bs: CONGRATULATIONS! You have a guy who truly cares about you.

Lots of Cs: OK, he might not be George Clooney, but he's a good guy and can only get better.

Lots of Ds: DELETE HIM! He's a self-centered jerk. Time to send him a farewell text and search for a type "A" guy!

CONCLUSION

We aren't doctors. We don't have specialized degrees in Relationships. And we don't have all the answers. But what we do have is years of experience, both our own and that of the many clients we have spent countless hours with working to understand what they go through, setting them up on dates, and coaching them in and out of love. Our mission in this book was to make sure that you'll never again check your voice mail twenty times a day after a date; that instead, you'll be confident when you meet a man for the first time. Also, we wanted to send the message that it's OK to be single; you don't need a man to be happy, but you do need to be happy with the man you finally choose.

A FINAL LOOK INSIDE THE MALE MIND: MAN-NERISMS: TRANSLATION PLEASE!

He says: "I would love to be intimate with you, but I don't want it to ruin our friendship."

He means: The thought of having sex with you is not appealing to me, but since I do enjoy hanging out, I am letting you down as gently as possible.

He says: "I don't mind if you go out with the girls. Seriously, have a great time tonight."

He means: I will be going out with the boys, either tonight or in the near future, and you won't be able to say anything about it.

He says: "Guys check you out all the time. I am so lucky to be with you."

He means: Please reassure me that you are not interested in anyone else. I have too much pride to ask.

He says: "I really love our time together."

He means: You are very special to me, and I want to keep seeing you.

He says: "Call me after girls' night out. I want to make sure you get home OK."

He means: I want to make sure you are in lockdown and home alone!

He says: "I meant to call you this weekend, but I lost track of time."

He means: I was with another woman or out with the guys, and I didn't have the opportunity to call.

He says: "Give me a call sometime."

He means: I am not interested enough to chase you, but you can chase me if you want to. I may or may not return your call.

He says: "I don't like to cuddle after sex."

He means: I have no problem sleeping with you, but I am not capable of displaying my emotional feelings at this point.

He says: "I would love to get married, but it's not the right time with where I am in my life."

He means: It will never be the right time, because you're not the right girl for me. So, I am using this pathetic excuse to buy myself more time until I meet someone.

(continued)

He says: "I am so unhappy at home. I wish my girlfriend/
wife were more like you."

He means: I want to sleep with you, and I don't want you to
feel guilty about it.

He says (on or before a first date): "I have never felt this
way before. You don't know how you make me feel; it's
driving me crazy."

He means: I have felt this way before, but I still REALLY
want to sleep with you.

RESOURCES

LOOKING YOUR BOND GIRL BEST

Looking your Bond Girl best takes a village. To help you put your best self forward, we've compiled a comprehensive list of resources and advice from our favorite top beauty and style gurus. It's all here, from products guaranteed to give you a shiny mane to undergarments designed to cover any figure flaw.

Bond Girl Hair

Yarokhair.com: If you're dealing with lifeless and dull hair, check out Yarok Hair Serum. It's a product that's specifically designed to make your hair shiny and give it body.

Phyto.com: Made with natural, botanical ingredients, this hair-care line will solve any hair problem from overprocessed locks to thinning hair to oily scalp.

Bond Girl Face

Labelladonna.com: This mineral-based makeup line offers a palette of colors and hues that will illuminate your face, giving you a seductive, natural-looking glow.

Poppyking.com: This lipstick line is pure genius. Whether you're wearing a shade from Poppy's Saint or Sinner line or her revolutionary Oxymoron line, your lips will look completely kissable.

Bethbenderbeauty.com: The fun, playful packaging of this makeup line is nearly as fantastic as the gorgeous, fresh makeup itself.

Bond Girl Bod

Spanx.com: On her site, Sara Blakely, the genius behind the Spanx undergarment line, offers a full assortment of bras, panties, and body shapers that will ensure that you're showing off your positives and hiding your negatives in any outfit.

Myintimacy.com: With her brilliant website and army of bra experts working in specialty boutiques around the country, bra-fitting guru Susan Nethero has started a full-on bra revolution.

Lindenleavesusa.com: These heavenly spa products will bring the services of that fancy day spa to you.

Bond Girl Fashion

Topbutton.com: This site is brimming with fabulous fashion advice. On top of that, it'll give you the inside scoop on all of the top designer clothing and fashion sample sales in the New York and L.A. metro areas.

Hollywoodfashiontape.com: Use this brilliant product to solve a multitude of fashion problems, such as slipping straps, falling hems, and gapping blouse fronts.

Pookieandsebastian.com: A fabulous resource for "first-date wear." Visit their four boutiques the next time you're in New York City.

Tamsen's Beauty Bag

These are my tried-and-true favorites:

Shu Uemura's eyelash curler: At eighteen dollars it is outrageously expensive for an eyelash curler, but I tell you, it changed my life. Make it one of your splurges: www.shu uemura-usa.com.

Fragrance Parvarti: A sexy, mysterious scent that keeps Matt intrigued: lakshminyc.com.

Smashbox Under Eye Brightener: Bye-bye dark circles! Visit smashbox.com.

Covergirl Lash Exact Mascara: I splurge on an eyelash curler, not mascara; Covergirl mascara can't be beat! Visit walgreens.com.

Mac Studio Fix Foundation: Gives me a flawless face anytime: maccosmetics.com.

Laura Mercier Lip Plumper: I love givin' my lips a pout out! Go to lauramercier.com.

Nars Lipstick in Red Lizard: For when I'm in the mood to vamp it up; this red lipstick is known for looking great on any skin tone: narscosmetics.com.

Benefit You're Bluffing: Gets rid of redness on the spot! Visit benefitcosmetics.com.

Estée Lauder Artist's Eye Pencil in SoftSmudge Black: The best eyeliner ever! Visit esteelauder.com.

Tarte Cheekstain: The best blush you can find! Go to tartecosmetics.com.

Beauty and the Blog

My five favorite beauty blogs keep me up to speed on all the current trends:

Themakeupgirl.typepad.com

Divasdressingroom.blogspot.com

http://libertylondongirl.blogspot.com

http://mrs-fashion.blogspot.com

Product-girl.com

Beautyblognetwork.com

INDEX

ABOUT THE AUTHORS

Matt Titus is the founder of Matt's Little Black Book, a Manhattan matchmaking agency that caters exclusively to the city's single, successful, and selective women. He works alongside his wife, Tamsen Fadal, to successfully guide singles in the city and help them find true love.

Matt has appeared on E! and The Style Network and is regularly featured on Fox's "The Morning Show with Mike and Juliet" as a relationship expert. He was a regular contributor to *Life & Style* magazine as the publication's "Love Doctor," answering questions about celebrity love lives.

Matt and Tamsen are featured in their own reality series, Lifetime's "Matt Titus: Matchmaker," which offers a behind-the-scenes look at their lives as successful "dating agents." They are also the founders of Sassybean.com, a website that spills the beans on life and love along with providing a weekly online magazine that offers honest insight from a real couple helping real women navigate the fun and sometimes frustrating world of dating.

A seasoned news journalist, **Tamsen Fadal** works alongside her husband, Matt Titus, as a relationship expert and dating coach. Tamsen not only adds a female perspective to Matt's advice and commentary, but also works with him to share the secrets of successful dating that helped them to become a couple.

Tamsen started as a journalist, most recently working as an on-air reporter/anchor at CBS's flagship station in New York City. She received an Emmy Award in 2005 for Outstanding Investigative Journalism and was also nominated for two Emmy Awards in 2004 for her investigative work. She has traveled to London to cover the U.K. bombings and to Afghanistan to cover the war on terror.

Tamsen writes a relationship column for a national woman's networking organization, Divas Who Dine, fielding questions from career women across the country. On a personal level she is active in causes to raise breast cancer awareness. After losing her mother to breast cancer in 1990, she has hosted several of the Susan G. Komen Foundation events for the disease and takes part in the annual walk.

Eddie Varley, illustrator: You've no doubt noticed the book's witty illustrations. Eddie Varley is responsible for these cartoons, which he also creates for our popular website sassybean.com. When he's not at the drawing table, Eddie pursues his successful career in musical theater on Broadway. He studied at both Tyler School of Art and the Art Institute of Philadelphia. His mom and dad are very happy he has picked up his crayons again.